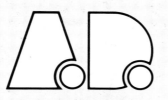

Architectural Design 55 9/10

Editorial Offices: 42 Leinster Gardens, London W2 Telephone: 01-402 2141 Subscriptions: 7/8 Holland Street London W8

EDITOR
Dr Andreas C Papadakis
HOUSE EDITOR: Frank Russell
CONSULTANTS: Catherine Cooke, Dennis Crompton, Terry Farrell, Kenneth Frampton,
Charles Jencks, Heinrich Klotz, Leon Krier, Robert Maxwell, Demetri Porphyrios, Colin Rowe, Derek Walker

Architectural Design Profile

DESIGNING A HOUSE

North-south section of the Thematic House

Influential critic and architect Charles Jencks began a three year collaboration with premiere British architect Terry Farrell in 1978 to transform a Victorian London terrace house into a 'built manifesto' of Post-Modernism. Rarely has a private house had so much care, design and theory lavished upon it, and the 'Thematic House' has already been the subject of a major book recently published by Academy Editions. This Profile is the first to publish in detail the process of design with a selection of the countless conceptual sketches, design drawings and working drawings which explain in detail how the house evolved. The addition of a two-storey annexe, paired interlocking conservatories, a central spiral staircase and mirrored lightshaft among other features created a dynamic space within which Jencks has applied a symbolic programme based on the cosmos, the solar system and the seasons, with the involvement of a variety of architects and artists including Michael Graves, Eduardo Paolozzi and Allen Jones. This *Architectural Design* Profile provides a rare, behind the scenes view of the intricate relationship between arch
accounts of the story of this unusual house's conception and d

Cover: Flying axonometric of the Thematic House by Charles Jencks: 'There is   C N Led
Architecture up among the whirlwinds and clouds that battle to dominate the sky',   face mot

A.D. Architectural Design Profile

Designing a House

BY CHARLES JENCKS AND TERRY FARRELL

TERRY FARRELL PARTNERSHIP
John Chatwin: Obtaining consents for planning, building regulations, etc
Tom Politowicz: Project architect September 1978–July 1979
David Quigley: Project architect July 1979–September 1980
Simon Husdpith: Project architect September 1980–December 1980
Simon Sturgis: Project architect December 1980–April 1982
Richard Solomon: Project architect April 1982–January 1983
(all the above were full-time in their commitment; other architects involved were Joe Foges,
Steve Marshall, Neil Porter)

INTERIORS AND FURNITURE
Charles Jencks

GARDEN DESIGN
Maggie Keswick

JACUZZI DESIGN
Piers Gough

INDIAN SUMMER AND AUTUMN WORKING DRAWINGS AND SUGGESTIONS
Johnny Grey Associates

WINTER AND SPRING FIREPLACES
Michael Graves

STRUCTURAL ENGINEER
David French

MAIN BUILDING CONTRACTORS
Hodgson Brothers: Stan Hodgson, John Brazier
On site: David Kitchener

SPECIALIST CARPENTER
Jack Culbert

ROOF WORK AND PAINTING
Eddie and Barnie O'Brien

SPECIALIST PAINTERS FOR INDIAN SUMMER, AUTUMN AND FURNITURE
Valentine Abbott, Wendy Baker, Pierre Beaudry, Jake Bowie, Paul and Janet Czainski,
Adrian Everitt, Sheila Sartin, Edgar Sirs, Dan Woodside

Charles Jencks

SYMBOLISM: THE NEXT STEP

THE NOTION OF PROGRESS IN THE ARTS IS A DEAD duck – no one believes that Rembrandt is a greater painter than Raphael because he came onto the evolutionary scene later. And yet, in limited ways that Giorgio Vasari and E H Gombrich have spelled out, this lifeless duck is in need of partial resuscitation. There are a few ways in which art can indeed improve as a result of its temporal position, as for example when one artist learns both technical and conceptual solutions from another and seeks to extend them. Only within a tradition, or a 'problem situation' as Karl Popper calls it, can one talk of progress and say, for instance, that Raphael improves the aerial perspective of Masaccio. Vitruvius places a great emphasis on progress in architecture, which he rightly attributes to imitation and competition – from the primitive hut to the Greek temple there is a continuing line of development, even if it is more mythical and conceptual than empirical.

Since Post-Modern architecture has become a recognised tradition over the past ten years, architects have begun to imitate and improve each other's solutions to the point where one can now speak of the 'standards' and 'monuments' of this movement. For example the notions of symbolic ornament developed by Italians such as Luigi Moretti in the 1950s were further articulated by Robert Venturi in the 1970s in the concept of the 'decorated shed' and then built in the 1980s, most convincingly by James Stirling (1,2).

Stirling and Wilford's Neue Staatsgalerie in Stuttgart uses high-tech ornament to symbolise all points of entry and circulation through a complex site, from the taxi drop-off point (a primitive hut in steel) to the lighting handrails and various doors.

The ornament not only tells the visitors how to navigate through this acropolis, but also tells them in different ways, some brash, others gentle. For example, blue-and-pink dayglo balustrades relate directly to the high-gloss polychromy that young visitors sport on their anoraks, while the Schinkelesque classicism relates directly to the traditionalists' idea of a museum. Stirling not only develops Venturi's idea of symbolic ornament, but also his notion of articulating the values of different 'taste-cultures'. With the Stuttgart gallery we can really speak of a building addressing itself to a plurality of groups – the 'radical eclecticism' I have been advocating for years. Modernist at the back, organic at the sides and doubly-coded at the front (De Stijl versus classicism), this building is the monument of Post-Modernism to date, the standard to surpass.

While this may all sound a bit portentous, the above judgement is no more subjective than to say that Raphael improved Masaccian perspective: it is an evaluation shared almost universally by critics in America, Japan and Germany because it refers to a limited truth. The Neue Staatsgalerie is richer in space and conception than Philip Johnson's AT&T building, it is better built than Michael Graves's Portland Public Service building, less cliché-ridden than Isozaki's Tsukuba Civic Centre or Bofill's palaces, more 'complex and contradictory' than Venturi's Gordon Wu Hall, and so on. This is not to say that it is perfect – the violent green rubber floors would be enough to dispel any notion of perfection even without the missing head or 'crown', solecisms that have not escaped criticism. But it does provide a valuable summing up of the Post-Modern notion that our reality is irreducibly plural, located as it is between the demands of the past

1

2

with its beauty and those of the present with its new technologies and struggle. Jean-François Lyotard identifies the struggle of 'language games' as the essence of *la condition post-moderne*; Stirling and Wilford, more convincingly than anyone else, have *built* this social reality.[1]

And yet if the Neue Staatsgalerie is the first fully mature representation of Post-Modernism (in terms of a comprehensible Free-Style Classicism), it also poses an obvious question for the next stage of development: what should be said in this shared language? On this question, the building is either woefully silent or else confused. When one walks around this acropolis and museum, one finds no ordered plot or scenario, no narrative thread to tie it all together. When I asked Stirling, as we gazed over his pantheon or sacred sculpture court (or ruin from Hadrian's Villa), just what occupied the centre of this round space, this 'holy of holies', he answered lamely, pointing to the hole in the middle, 'a drain' (3). And what then did the twelve holes cut into the three circles signify — the Trinity? 'No, the cross-section of an electric cable.' This answer, rather like Henry Adams's prediction that the Dynamo would replace the Virgin of Chartres, at least *was* an answer and we should be thankful for that, however nihilistic or inconsequential it might be. Most architects don't give symbolism a thought, least of all when dealing with their plumbing details.

But if Stirling had thought about the significance of his twelve black holes (or at least guessed that I would ask him), he certainly failed to place this Dadaist gesture in a narrative in which it would be a carefully conceived crescendo (or anti-climax) to a plot. Instead it was yet another meaning dropped onto a collage. And while Colin Rowe's *Collage City* – like Venturi's 'decorated shed' – is an important stage in formulating a Post-Modern urbanism, it can also lead to evasions. When taken as a complete prescription for design, the collage approach allows one to overlook the interrelation of parts, the planned interaction of meaning. It's too easy to collage signs and symbols together, just as it's ultimately trivial to stick them on a decorated shed.

Symbols are only symbols if they *resonate* (and don't clang) and the only way they can resonate is if their overtones are worked through. The architect must design so that everyday meanings – drains and the like – can relate to or contrast with more important meanings, social, political and religious. This, of course, is an onerous duty in an agnostic society (which doesn't even tell the architect what to censure), but not an impossible one. The architect can find numerous hints for a lead in a functional programme and he can also, I would suggest, consciously write up

symbolic programmes with his client which will make the goals more explicit. Had Stirling and the Stuttgart authorities written up such programmes, they would have been forced to confront certain anomalies in their scheme such as the discrepancy between the circulation route and the sequence of the art. The pressing question – what should architecture express? – can only be answered by both client and architect together and will continue to be evaded in our society unless they are expected to answer it. To draw up an iconographic programme or contract would force them into an existential confrontation with such questions, where they have to answer for the public meaning of architecture.

In the Thematic House, the subject of this issue, we often designed to such programmes, or had them vaguely in mind. I believe that they not only liberate the designer to ornament, but to ornament in a way which transcends the decorated shed or the discordant collage. Because the craftsman, artist, interior designer and architect all know roughly what the meaning of a room is, then they are able more confidently to express their particular arts. The iconographic programme, in providing an overall narrative, unifies the parts of the building on the level of content. It is the individual designer's role to unify, or collage, the levels of form.

The iconographic programme is an idea which can probably be traced back through thousands of years of neo-Platonism to the Egyptian priests of the Old Kingdom; it only seems new to us today because it hasn't been practised since the turn of the century. At that time one could find many architects as various as Frank Lloyd Wright, Antonio Gaudí and Hector Guimard working with symbolic ideas; they may not have written them down, but these ideas obviously crossed and recrossed their minds. The justification for producing an explicit iconographic contract today is that it would help focus the client and architect's mind on an area which would, in an agnostic society, otherwise be surpressed. And this repression, as Freud, Jung and so many others have warned us, can end by kicking us up the subconscious.

* * *

The following drawings and comments on the Thematic House show some of the many stages we went through in trying to reconcile the symbolism with functional and formal concerns. It would be presumptuous to claim that this reconciliation has occurred in all cases and that the result is the resonant symbolism which I advocate as the goal of design: however, this is and was the long-term intention. The narrative programmes are not included, nor detailed descriptions, which can be found in *Towards a Symbolic Architecture* (Academy Editions, 1985). The one exception to this rule, the Room of Doubles, is presented next with its original symbolic programme and a final description to bring out both the attainments and difficulties of symbolic design. Following this are sections on some of the design stages where I have been able to reconstruct them. This process is not complete partly because so many drawings are not available, or not shown.

1 Jean-François Lyotard *The Post-Modern Condition: a Report on Knowledge* Manchester University Press 1984 (first published in France, 1979).

1, 2 James Stirling, Michael Wilford Associates *Neue Staatsgalerie* Stuttgart 1977-84. The polychromatic steel temple marks the taxi drop-off point and the colourful lighting handrails indicate the route – an imaginative transformation of Venturi's decorated shed. (Jencks)
3 *Neue Staatsgalerie* outdoor sculpture court. The wonderful 'sacred space' focuses not on an altar but on a drain. (Jencks)

3

1

THE ROOM OF DOUBLES

As the symbolic programme for this basement room makes clear, the Room of Doubles was first conceived as a traditional garden room – a *sala terena* taking on aspects of nature, greenery and rusticity appropriate to garden activity. As usual this programme was written near the beginning of design and not everything was carried out, but it is quoted in full to give an idea, together with some of the early sketches, of the way symbolic goals are first specified.

INITIAL PROGRAMME FOR THE ROOM OF DOUBLES, APRIL 1985
The two rooms on either side of the jacuzzi open directly onto the garden and should have a garden-like atmosphere full of trees, trellis, insects, flowers, bees and birds – or their representation.

A cool set of greens should provide the background, as it does in the traditional sala terena, as a respite from the summer heat. The hues should be spring-like having a yellow or light green tone like the early leaves. Apple green should be set against the darker green of the ground. The sky, full of birds, could undulate in a mysterious way, as if clouds were pushing down over mountains as a weather front moved in.

What exactly this undulating dado should hold – trees, birds, mountainscape – is open to discussion. But the objects placed against the green background should come forward and have recesses in blue, like views through the sky – to create ambiguity and a layering effect.

Mystery could also be created by the strange scale of the paired animal objects. Everything should come

2

in twos, like Noah's Ark. The Room of Doubles should be symmetrical everywhere one looks and have objects doubled wherever possible. This geometry might be underscored by the carpet, ceiling, lettering and numbering: 1 & 2, First & Second, Male and Female, Yang and Yin etc.

The room as built did not include the stencils of trees, birds and mountains because when we tried these images on the walls they became too complicated. An early sketch (1) shows the room with an overlay of bird parts – mainly heads apart from the moving wings of a flamingo flying (which would make a very interesting frieze). Some of these features were incorporated into the twin 'owl' cupboards and

headboard. Opposite this are two more cheerful cupboards, smiling gnomes, which hold sliding boxes for storing children's toys (2). These doubles are placed on either side of a double door. The ceiling overhead has two mirror 'eyes' and is painted two different shades of blue and the carpet is also doubled (3,4). A large wall mirror reflects the view to the garden and further pairs of objects (5,6); indeed, the greens of the room could even be seen as doubling the greens of the garden. Throughout the room rather obvious children's imagery is countered by the abstract shapes of a guest room. And as the sofa is convertible into a bed, the Room of Doubles has a double function as a playroom and spare bedroom.

3

4

Charles Jencks

THE THEMATIC HOUSE
The Design Process

'To name an object is to suppress three-fourths of the enjoyment . . . to suggest it, that is the dream.'
Gauguin on Mallarmé's theory of symbolism

'La Nature est un temple où de vivants piliers/Laissent parfois sortir de confuses paroles;/L'homme y passe à travers des forêts de symboles/Qui l'observent avec des regards familiers.' Charles Baudelaire,
'Correspondances', *Les Fleurs du Mal*

1

THE DESIGN OF THE THEMATIC HOUSE EVOLVED over many years. As I have described the symbolism of the interiors extensively elsewhere, I will concentrate here on the architecture and spaces. Like other work of mine, this house was intended partly as a trial of and polemic on symbolic architecture and this may explain some of its more unusual aspects. Polemical buildings tend to be overdesigned, if not overwrought, to prove a point or test an idea – here the notion that every room or piece of furniture should be part of a symbolic programme in order to give point and unity to visual expression and ornament. The intention was for a symbolic not a signolic architecture.[1]

I should emphasise, however, that the building did *evolve* and was not preconceived in every symbolic detail. At first it was vaguely called the Solar House because of projected sun collectors on the roof and its south-facing conservatories; when Maggie Keswick and I worked with Terry Farrell and his team, it was called the Terrace House because of its three main terrace connections and its place as part of the tradition of the London terrace house; later still it was called the Time House because of the emphasis on cultural and cosmic time – for instance the spiral galaxies represented throughout and the spiral stair. So, as with most symbolic architecture, it was as much a question of discovering latent symbolism as of imposing an *a priori* programme. Because of this complex evolution, it is often hard to give precise credits where they are due, although I have tried to do this in the *Terry Farrell Monograph* and *Towards a Symbolic Architecture*.[2] Originally I had intended that Terry and I should set out, date and order all the drawings and come to common conclusions, but this has not yet proved possible with the result that there may be some contradictions between our two accounts. For example, he clearly remembers conceiving the notion of the Four Seasons as the ordering principle of the ground floor, while I, just as clearly, remember thinking of the idea after I had seen the plan of J F Neufforge's 'Bâtiment à representer les quatres saisons ou les quatre éléments' which also centres on a circular staircase (1). Maggie has other memories still, so maybe it's a case of simultaneous invention. In any case, it is certainly true that several key designs were produced in close collaboration with others – the staircase, library, fireplaces and jacuzzi come immediately to mind, as well as a host of structural details worked out by our craftsmen Steve Agombar and John Longhurst. Since this issue of *Architectural Design* is concerned with the architecture, however, I will only concentrate on the building design.

THE SOLAR HOUSE
June-October 1978

The house was bought in May 1978. Its previous owner, an elderly woman, had done only basic maintenance for many years. Some original features and parts of the mouldings had disappeared, and the garage/studio which she had added in the 1950s was not connected to the main house. Some of the basic structure, such as the dormers and main windows, remained the essential location for later design (2). In June, at the recommendation of Nicky Johnson, Maggie and I went to Michael Fisher of Fisher Associates with the idea that we would design the house and he would detail and carry out our plans.

We started with two basic ideas. The first was that the front of the building should be related to its context in the street. Hence the many drawings of the 'rabbit' balusters, chimney shapes, dormer windows, etc. which are described as 'local motifs' in the several sketches (3). The second main idea was spatial – that we should use double-height spaces, arcades to the garden and a sequence of stairs and terraces. These surround glazed conservatories, some of which run the whole height of the building, while others rise up only half way (4). Many of these ideas were incorporated in the built version, although the western addition as built is one storey lower. Even here, however, the notion of a stylised face has been salvaged from the first designs (5).

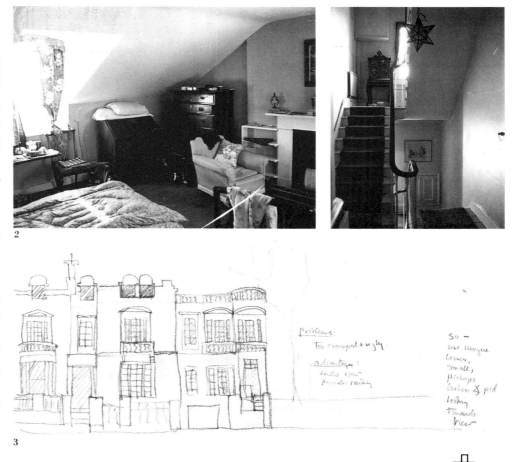

2

3

1 Jean-François Neufforge, 'Bâtiment à representer les quatres saisons . . .' (from *Recueil élémentaire d'architecture*, 1777), shows the logical disposition around a central stair. The classical grammar is interlocked like a rigorous puzzle.
2 Views of the pre-existing structure show the smaller dormers and the way sunlight and the garden are blocked by the staircase. The initial idea was to open up the house to the views and allow the sun to penetrate everywhere – a Solar House.
3 One of the eight 'quick-logic' elevations to see the problems created by extending the existing grammar of 'rabbits', dormers and sash windows. The basic intention was to complete the row of three houses so that it would read as a unity, with slight differences (for example, the dormers cut into the cornice).
4 One of six 'quick-logic' elevations of the south facade. This scheme shows the conservatories which step back in plan and form a unifying presence. Various studies of baroque (and broken) pediments and staggers were made in an attempt to give the glass walls a shimmering effect. The built version has many of the qualities of this first elevation including the stepped shapes below the pediments.

4

The interior planning was quite a complex mixture of classical demi-forms (half ovals, fragmented primary shapes) and Modernist open planning. This Post-Modern hybrid was the expression of one of those polemical points mentioned above, perhaps in this case over-emphasised since every room flows into another yet is still partly centred by ceiling beams and lights (the dotted lines in the plan, 6). What is apparent from this initial plan is the general bay rhythm (from left to right, ABBA) which remained the ordering principle in all later schemes, together with the primary functional placement, which has also remained substantially the same. Maggie thought of moving the stairs from the southern garden facade, where they would block the view and light, so that in my scheme they became 'C' and 'K' initials in plan, while in hers they are located in two places – one of which is the centre of the house where they have remained (7). Another feature of these first plans which was realised in modified form was the use of columns and walls to order the sequence to the garden. At first these were London columns marching down the axis, holding up the previous wall loads and setting up cross-over axes which focus on the two main fireplaces. This alternation of major and minor axes has been built, but with a wall of 'windows on the world' and mirrors on the ceiling.

The initial plans for the first floor also show a functional zoning similar to the final result except that what is indicated as a spare bedroom was to become Maggie's study, and the central stairwell had not yet been designed (8). Present, however, is the fourposter bed in the main bedroom and the bath looking over the garden and connected acoustically to the bedroom (an idea which implies more traditional ideas of bathing than Modernist notions of

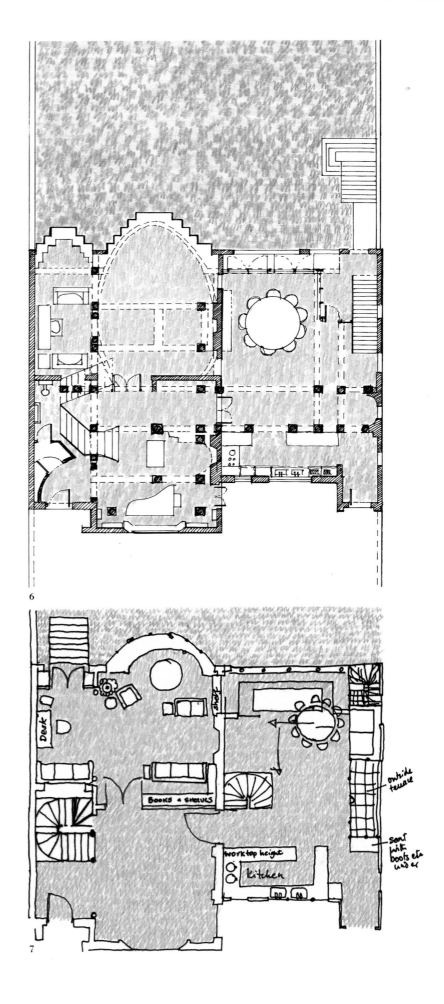

6

5

5 Sketch of the west facade showing one of several versions of the 'face' focusing on the 'sun altar' at the top; also present is the idea of using 'windows on the world' as eyes.
6 The ground floor is opened up as the western wall is cut at points. The idea of space flowing around the two *focii*, the chimneys, is also present here. The staircase, alternating 'C's and 'K's, continues the entrance oval form; the dining room opens over a double-height space.
7 The ground floor in Maggie's version shows a central staircase and outside terrace, later to be realised in a different form. She wanted more lateral connections of rooms than we finally achieved.

7

getting clean in a dark hole).[3] The terrace opening off the library was built in the end, but what was finally lost was the idea of a stairway running through the whole house connecting all these floors with the garden. The section and other plans also show large openings to the garden and enlarged dormer windows – all elements which played out the idea of the Solar House oriented to the wide garden view (9). It was this aspect that recommended the site to Maggie in the first place.

By October, with the rough design clear and the house laid out, it became obvious that Michael Fisher's office wasn't large enough to carry through all these complex intentions. We discussed who might help us and Maggie suggested Terry Farrell. Earlier I had asked him to lecture at the Architectural Association and at a RIBA summer conference and I knew him to be flexible and interested in collaborating with others. In addition, his technical expertise and building experience would compensate for our weaknesses in those areas. I showed him my drawings, some of which are illustrated here, and mentioned that we wanted to design as a group with him. Specifically, I asked if I could use his office, or a draughtsman in it, and he kindly agreed – a situation which worked for the next three years with David Quigley, Simon Sturgis and Richard Solomon in turn working with us and overseeing the construction work.

Footnotes

1 See 'Symbolic or Signolic Architecture?', *Art & Design* October 1985, pp. 14-19, 48.
2 See *Terry Farrell*, Academy Editions 1985, p. 148 and *Towards a Symbolic Architecture*, Academy Editions 1985, pp. 242-45.
3 See S. Giedion, *Mechanization Takes Command*, Oxford University Press 1948, especially pp. 706-11 for a critique of this trend.

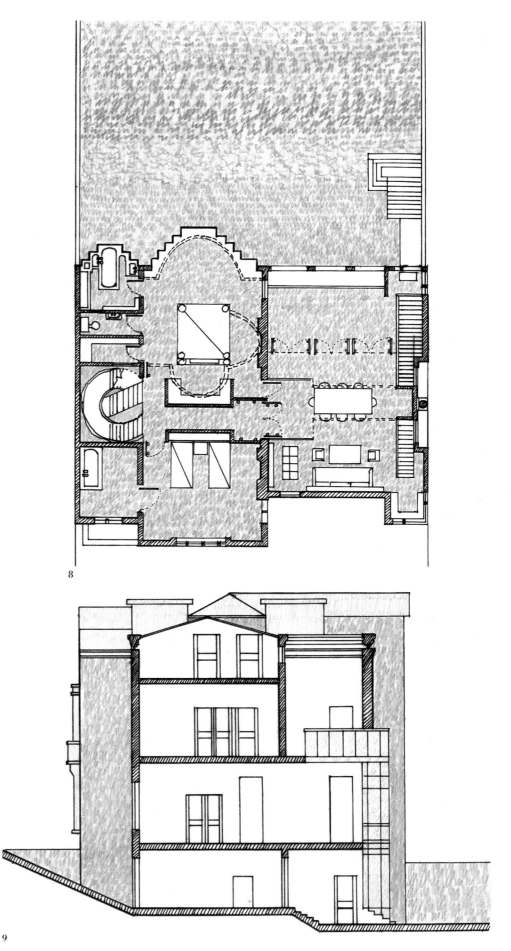

8

8 The first floor shows a continuation of the baroque demi-forms and the use of double doorknobs in a decorative manner to centralise views. In this version the library opens onto a terrace without the conservatory coming through, and a stairway runs clear from top to garden.
9 The section shows the conservatory cutting into the first floor terrace; later it was doubled and integrated spatially.

9

THE TERRACE HOUSE
Collaboration with Terry Farrell
October 1978-February 1979

The second stage of design, with Terry Farrell, began in mid-October 1978 and continued at a very intense level with weekly meetings for two months. At these meetings, Terry, Maggie, David Quigley and I would all design together, or in sequence, sometimes even having an internal four-way 'race' to see who could design the best solution to a problem. In January I went to Los Angeles to teach and we carried on design through airmail letters and drawings, reaching a near-final development by 19 February 1979 – as quotes from my letter of that date, below, make clear.

The most significant accomplishments of this second stage were the reduction of the study addition – Terry's ingenious idea to satisfy planning requirements – and working out the centralised stairway, an elaboration of Maggie's initial idea. The open planning and spatial ideas were a development of the first scheme, the Solar House. Sometime during the initial two months of collaboration we hit on the idea of using the Four Seasons as a symbolic programme; they can be seen written on several of my plans and on top of Terry's. Other symbolic ideas can also be seen in embryonic form: the London columns which focus diagonal views; an ornament based on Maggie's and my initials (which came to nothing in the end); the face motif or Jencksiana as the 'family of forms'; the 'windows on the world' leading to the garden; and above all the idea of connecting levels – the terraces of the Terrace House. Our rejection of this name and symbolic programme in the end was partly because it was too complicated to get from one terrace to the next and finally to the garden. But the three terraces did remain in the final design, although unconnected – a typical example of how a major idea sometimes ends up as a vestigial remnant.

It is most convenient to discuss the sequence of the design drawing by drawing in so far as I've been able to reconstruct it, although some drawings are missing and the sequence is not always clear. The two major ideas – the reduced study addition and the semi-open plan – will be analysed in turn.

THE STUDY ADDITION

By the end of November, after Terry had proposed that we cut down the height of the addition by shrinking the kitchen and study ceilings, I made a sequence of four drawings, one of which was called 'minimum solution with crown' (1). This shows the 'problem of scale and character change' (the fact that the row of three houses would suddenly drop in height and change character). As can be seen, I didn't know how to handle the central stair

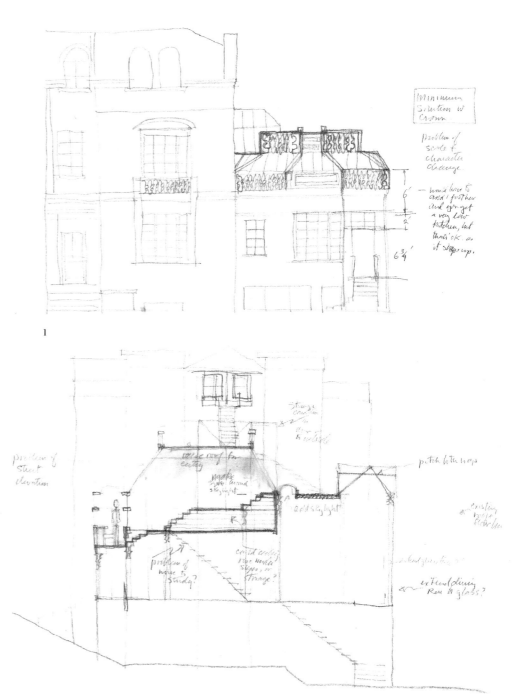

1

2

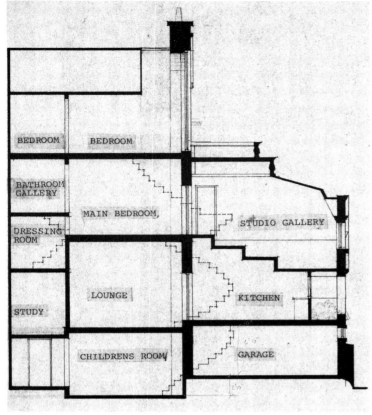

3

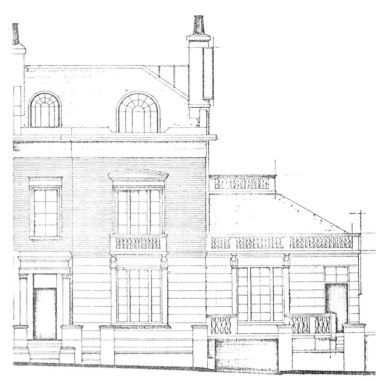

4

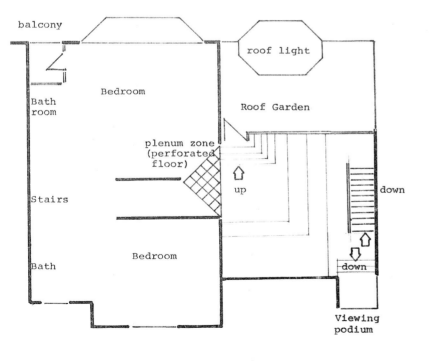

FIRST FLOOR ALTERNATIVE: A STEPPED STUDY

5

and its connection to the library – a glazed connection is shown – but I had imagined that the low height of the kitchen could be handled by steps. This can be seen from the marginal notes and the stepped section (2), which rises in space and light towards the garden. Also on this section is a note about using these steps 'as a theatre for projecting slides and a lecture room', an idea which was realised in the Architectural Library.

Terry took this section one stage further, although he stepped it towards the side elevation rather than the garden (3). What was finally built – steps which rise towards the street and a big space over the dining room – was therefore transformed from these tentative solutions. Characteristically, two or three opposing schemes were tried before the result was synthesised. As can be seen from Terry's schematic drawings, one version of the study stepped away from the roof garden and central 'plenum zone' (the staircase was to be the 'central heating' in a literal sense), that is, stepped both north and west (4). This solution obviously proved how unworkable my idea would be, since the large amount of stair space compromises the study (2). We had, however, come to a generalised solution when Terry turned my steps to the north and cut out those to the south and west. The resultant street facade (February 1979) shows the kind of synthesis we had reached (5). The 'rabbit' balconies remain from the very first scheme and much else from this scheme was also finally built including the rustication, and the duplication of the main window. The next important steps were to cut the dormers into the cornice, relocate the central stairwell, and doubly curve the study roof.

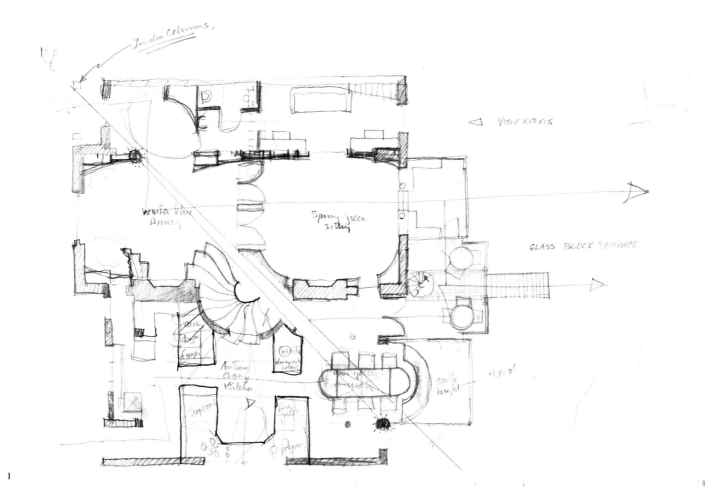

1

THE SEMI-OPEN PLAN

The initial idea of spatial planning that Maggie and I had when we first bought the house was to open up vistas wherever possible. Light, space and views were to us the obvious goals – a complex web of continuous space which could be interrupted in parts, closed down to a few feet in others, and framed by openings as in a Chinese garden; but it would nevertheless remain continuous space which would extend the eye and imagination. The space developed from this hybrid baroque and Modern notion would then be controlled by rooms which would be essentially closed and classical in form. Axes, cross axes and simple geometrical forms would exist in plan and on the ceiling, to be violated only at small points. The result was the 'semi-open plan', or use of 'demi-classical forms', as we called them.

One of my drawings (1) shows some of the essential ideas – the fragmented classical shapes and important diagonal axis connecting the two London columns (a diagonal which makes this space unusual for a London terrace house). The routes to the garden are shown as arrows which follow the 'shifted axis' typical of the Parisian hôtel. These hôtels were located between the busy street and the quiet garden and to make this transition more pleasant and dramatic the path between the two would be displaced once or twice to culminate in a terrace view – as here. The drawing also shows the major functional spaces as finally built, here with their colours ('winter blue drawing', 'spring green sitting',

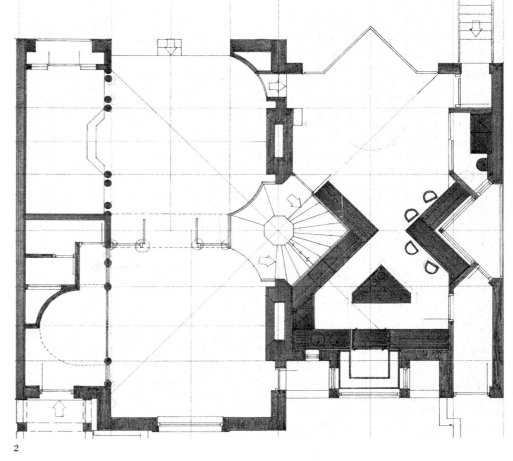

2

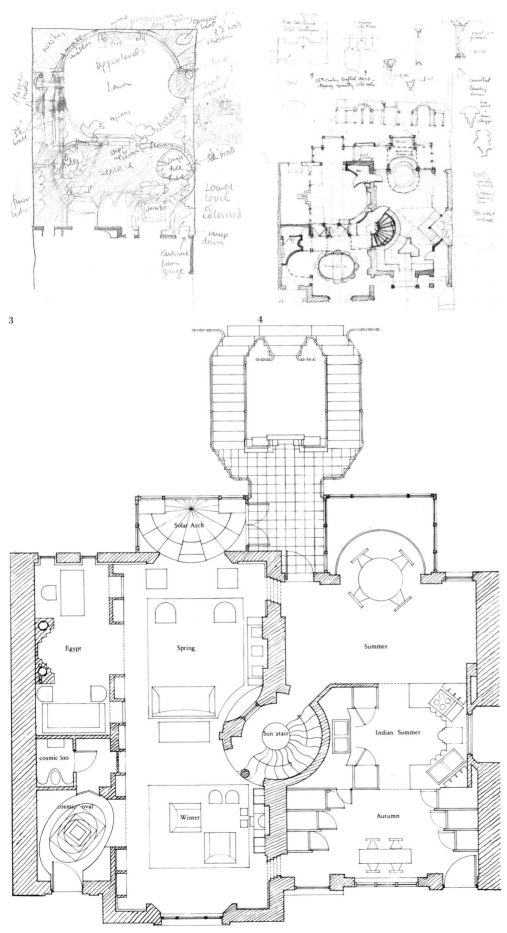

3

4

5

'summer yellow conservatory', etc., although 'autumn orange kitchen' was later to be changed). The curving sunrays of the stair are evident, as is its interpenetration into different rooms to be picked up in the ceiling beams of the kitchen. Also present is the wall of books – 'windows on the world' – which was given a slight and unifying curve at cornice level. This and the single stair to the garden were not built, but in most other respects this plan was carried out.

Terry's versions of the ground floor contained angular forms which Maggie found too pinching in the kitchen area (2). Both Terry and I also experimented with rather complicated routes through the back of the kitchen that didn't finally work. Maggie was designing the garden at this time, and an early sketch of hers shows how it was meant to carry out the aB bay rhythm of the house (3). Also present are the upper level lawn and lower level terrace, as well as the central focus of the mirror at the end. The jacuzzi was later to move to the centre and a continuous brick path, for cycling, was added.

When I was in Los Angeles, I sent Terry a further plan and letter, 19 February, which pushed the arguments forward in some respects and backwards in others (4). The letter makes certain points, among others:

'. . . 1) The windows should be roughly 30% openable – so I have designed a south elevation which is divided into 3 main bays which each have a center bay for viewing and side bays for opening . . . [This tripartite organisation was built, but the side windows don't open.]

'3) I'm trying to develop the shifted axis since opposite facades don't always line up. There are some 18th century precedents (Hôtels Matignon and Rohan in Paris). Thing is to keep symmetry but shift it: asymmetrical symmetry.

'4) The stairs I've tried to organize as discs that slide over each other leaving residual space inside and out . . .

'5) The round columns are going to be so expensive, I thought of reinventing the I-beam out of wood and slapping on a head (capital) and shoe (base), and making up the web out of bits of wood. We could invent L, and U and T beams to which, with these heads and shoes would resemble pilasters, and they would go around corners a lot easier than columns . . .' These pilasters are shown at the top of the drawing (4) and although they were never built, the ideas of the London columns and the face motif were derived from them. One can see the 'feminine curves and masculine staggers' labelled in the drawings.

In all these plans the large dining table is shown in Winter, to be moved from Summer and expanded by adding a central leaf. Although this and the door divisions between Winter and Spring were never built, it is interesting to see how close this plan of February is to the final version (5). Other changes include the reduction of the conservatory space to two glazed areas and the connection of Autumn with Winter. Thus in the first four months of collaborative design we had arrived at all the major spatial ideas, which were not to be elaborated until three years later when interior design was to start again.

THE REAR FACADE
November 1978-March 1981

The rear garden facade of a typical London terrace house is usually a mess of pipes and stray windows. Ours was no exception (1). The small dormer window wasn't centred over the protruding bay window and the small windows giving light to the stairway didn't even have a picturesque charm. Hence my first elevations of the Solar House tried to pull all this together into three main vertical bays.

After we met Terry in November, he suggested that we unify the vertical conservatories and combine them to give passive solar heating which would be transferred to a 'heat store' in the centre of the house. Ralph Lebens was consulted and he produced studies which showed how this south-facing conservatory could work efficiently if it was large enough. Hence my next set of rear facade studies – and I made over fifty of them during the two-year period – show the integration of two small towers with a glazed link between them.

Two of eight elevations produced soon after we met show the solutions as half-symbolic and half-formal. 'Aedicules and screens' (2) was an attempt to unify the rear facade by using pitched roofs, or aedicules, and a grid of screened glass. It is not a happy solution as the right-hand area remains unintegrated, but it does show several important ideas – for example, the balcony decoration made from our initials – 'C', 'J', 'M', 'K', etc.; the arch pediment which focuses the view from the study; and two bridges leading out to the garden from Spring and Summer. All these ideas except the initials were to be transformed into the final design – for example, the bridges to the garden do lead, roughly, from these two seasons. Another of the eight proposals is called 'Foreground faces and background' (3) and here we can discern an important idea that was finally realised – the notion that the two conservatories should symbolise two faces which might then be transformed in the background. The Jencksiana – the curve and stagger motif – became at this time an organisational principle, one which I had used in previous designs and at an exhibition on Post-Modernism in 1977. The virtues of this motif are that it can be stretched and distorted – like a Serliana – and that it resembles significant things, for example a tree or a human face. Like a Chinese gate it also focuses and centralises the view.

At the same time as I was drawing up these rear facades, Terry was also producing his versions, which incorporate several of the same ideas – for example, the major and minor conservatories and the unified small towers (4). His additions tended to be more like the abstract glazed grids he was building elsewhere than my versions with mouldings, and they had the same problems as my own studies in failing to resolve the right-hand windows. A small step forward was made in my design of 19 February 1979, alluded to in the letter quoted above – here the curve of the face motif was integrated with the curve of the roof (5). I had thought of curving this roof in the manner of the 'Hildebrandtian

1

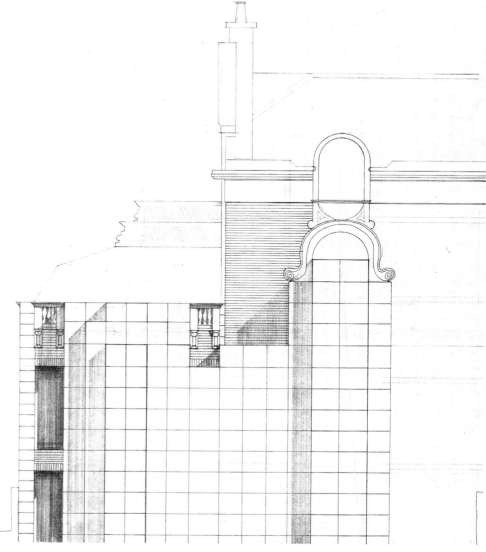

4

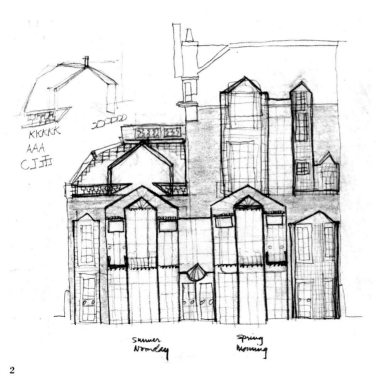

KKKKK
AAA
CJ田

J K

Summer
Noonday

Spring
Morning

2

3

5

6

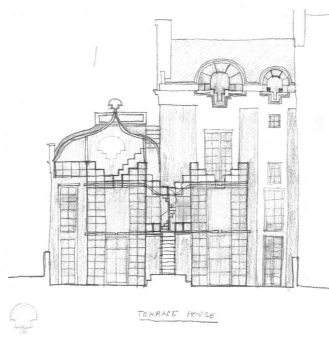

TERRACE HOUSE

7

Parten with mapesworth Terrace
Paragraph (stockside + see where holes
are g another lift + right window symmetrical
14 June 1980

motif' (a double curve which Lucas von Hilde-brandt used in the early eighteenth century) to lessen the jarring transition to the top balcony, and Terry mentioned that the curve in steel would not cost more than the straight sections. Maggie determined that the left-over shape of this curve could be a Gothic ogee, and so it is partly shown in this drawing. Another of our intentions in using the face motif was to repeat similar forms throughout the house, as the let-ter explains: '2) The arch above the left bay is symbolic and frames the view: it is free-stand-ing and should relate to graduated or staggered cut-outs behind (i.e. frame into them). I'm trying to develop a family of forms based on the shallow curve and stagger . . . if you remember our cut-out in Park Walk.'

Terry then built a model of the library with a double curved roof to show the implications for the interior space and structure (6). From this derived the nine ribs of the major space, which later became a pretext for the nine planet lights. Combined with Maggie's notion of the ogee, it also led to a visual crisis where all the ceiling lines came to a point. To try to solve this, and still retain the connected terraces, I produced a design on 14 June 1980 which had the double curves end in the face motif (7). This design, called the Terrace House because it connected the four major terraces, was not an adequate solution, but it nonetheless represented a breakthrough to the final versions because of two things – firstly, it finally unified the right-hand windows under a face motif and stucco body and secondly it acknowledged the double curves as symbolic and expressive *focii*. This led to a host of ideas for symbolic elements to be placed there – including keystones, faces, palm fronds, plants, urns and caryatids designed by my sister – none of which came to fruition. But the split of the conservatories and the unifica-tion of the vertical bays were retained in the

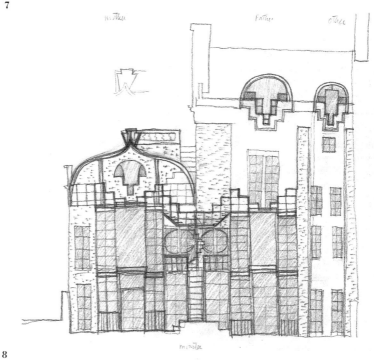

8

built solution. In another drawing made at this time (8) I saw them as members of a family ('mother', 'father', 'other', 'monster' – this last being the dog in the basement).

Terry built a model of this drawing which showed, more or less, how complicated the terrace connections would be, especially in the top and middle sections (9). This model also started to show the difficulties of relating the rear and side elevations. My answer to the former problem was a set of drawings produced by 18 July 1980 and sent to Terry with a letter: 'Enclosed are three drawings of the three facades – you'll see that they don't always match up which is part of the glory of architecture. What I like about them is their difference – as you go around the building, its

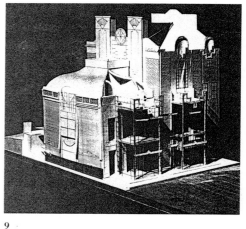

9

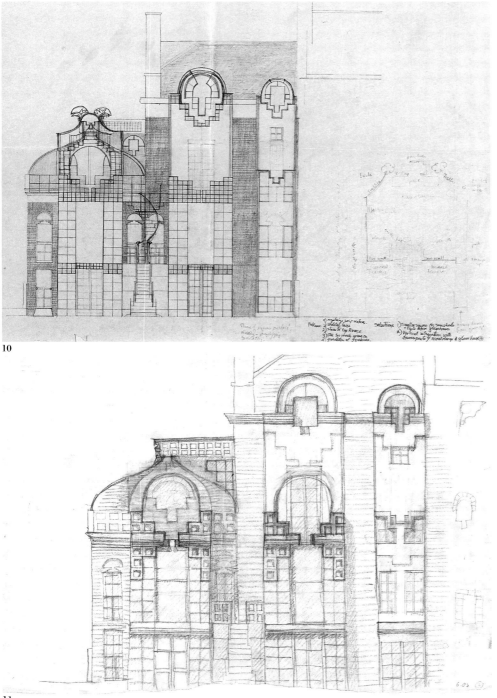

10

13

11

12

meaning changes rather like one of those trick billboards with the different vertical divisions.' The idea was that the meanings of the three facades would become more personal as one went from public street to private garden (10). These designs also brought to light some 'problems' which I enumerated in the letter and marginal commentary: the faces were too 'skeletal' or death-like in appearance, a problem that was ultimately lessened when I designed steel 'haloes' for their heads; there was 'still too much going on', a problem lessened by cutting out the palm ornament, the terrace connections and minor grids. The major advance made in this drawing was the ommission of the central conservatory and the integration of the downspouts and mouldings in a single

language.

The next advances were small ones, made in coloured drawings I did in September, which show the articulation of 'bird' images in the dormer windows (11). The stucco was to be layered here to give small set-backs which transformed the face image into a face-plus-tiny-body (12). These bird images symbolised the 'two children', as opposed to the large conservatories which were seen to become the 'mother and father'. And while the general notion of symbolising a family in the rear elevation had been present for four months, it was the small 'birds' which forced this symbol to be treated in the conservatories, albeit implicitly rather than explicitly. Indeed my intention throughout the design was to veil the symbols of the family by combining them with familiar abstract forms such as the arch. A recognisable human form at such scale would quickly have become trite and oppressive.

The next stage in the design occurred in October 1980 when I drew up an axonometric. This drawing is very close to the final design and resolves the two visible facades and the relation to the garden (13). My idea in drawing an axonometric was to pull several questions together in one drawing where they could be discussed in relation to each other: for instance the 'birds', 'faces', terraces, downspouts and double stair. When we met and discussed this drawing, Joe Foges, a new member of Terry's team, suggested that the window walls might be openable like giant sash windows. This notion appealed to all of us because it allowed better access, both literal and visual, to the garden, and also because it simplified the language equating the giant and small sash windows. Soon after this we were informed that for fire reasons the conservatories would have to be made in concrete, and thus their appearance became heavier.

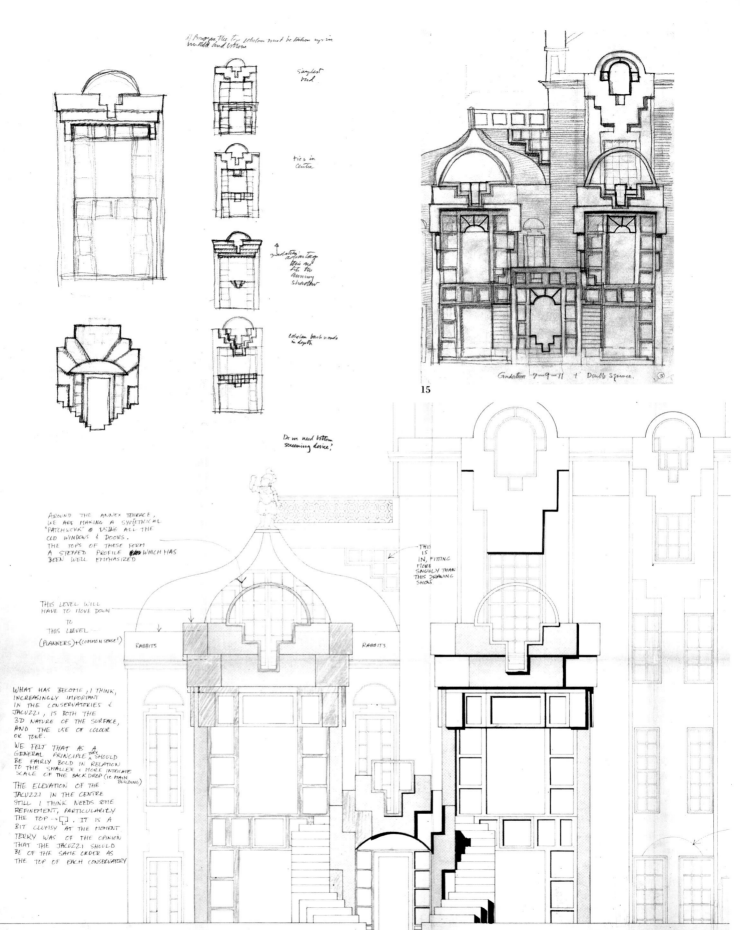

My response to this was a set of 'quick-logic' sketches and two elevations of the conservatories. The sketches (14) show the 'bird' image pulling together the centre of the echelons much as the two dormer windows were tied in. They also show each conservatory as a human body – the 'mother and father' – and the jacuzzi as a stepped keystone. Simon Sturgis or Terry later made the keystone into a steel void, something that lessened its weight. The elevations I made at this time were slightly more explicit bodies than were finally built, with exaggerated shoulders and feet (15). By now, November 1980, the double stair was designed to wrap around the jacuzzi.

Things remained more or less at this stage until Terry produced his final elevation drawing in February 1981, a version of which was sent to me with comments by Simon (16). This shows only minor changes from my drawings, as well as some incidental points – a small figure is placed at the top of the ogee while below this a 'patchwork' of windows and doors is used on the library. Simon felt, as his marginal comments make clear, that 'colour and tone' should modulate the conservatories and that the top of the jacuzzi was a bit 'clumsy'. I felt the window rhythm could be improved both at the top and through the 'belt' of the body, and also that the jacuzzi could be simplified with baroque setbacks. My letter of 3 March 1981 outlines my response to the two drawings: 'Enclosed are some immediate responses to the rear elevations showing alternatives (a)[17] and (b)[18] of which we prefer (a). As you can see it gets the transformation of the bird image into each "tower"; it is fairly simple and gets the layering in you have shown. Also the jacuzzi shape is simpler, but incorporates the baroque (or is it Art Deco?) setbacks. All in all I think we are getting very close to the final solution.'

In fact we were there – all Simon had to do now was layer the bird and the 'horizontal' solution together and void the keystone (19). More than two years of design and fifty elevations had been necessary to resolve the technical, functional, formal and symbolic intentions. They are resolved, I believe, in the sense that a fairly simple grammer of white trim and white echelons forms the foreground figures (the five bodies) in front of the background brick. The stairs don't obtrude too much, nor entirely destroy these figures, because of their lightness and transparency. Some may find the rear facade too fussy, but for me the figures have a noble yet quite personal presence.

19

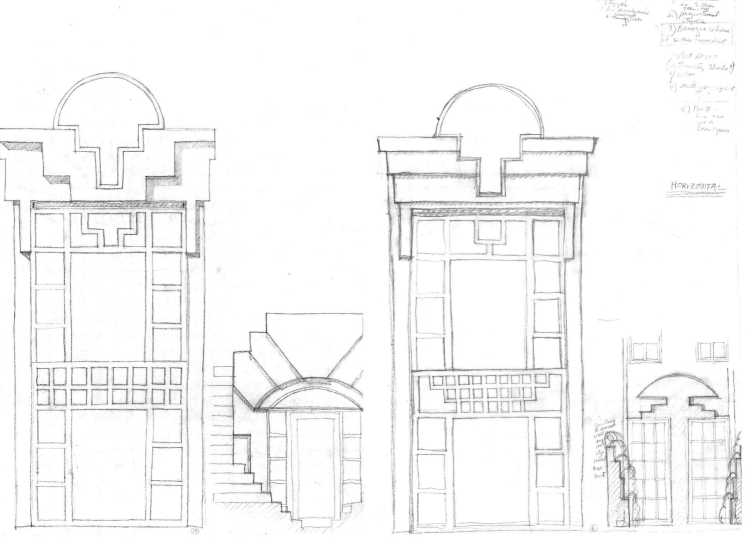

17

18

23

1

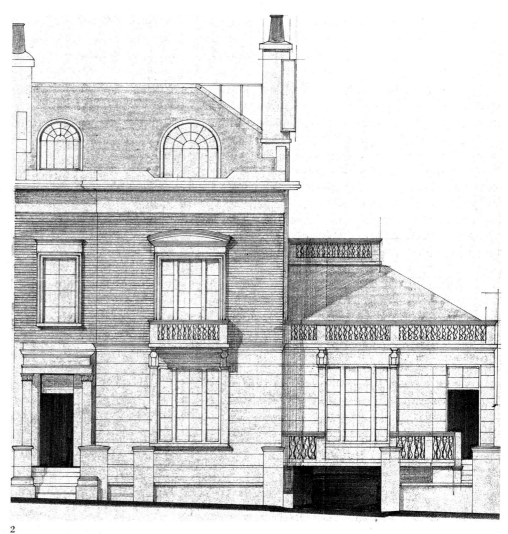

2

THE FRONT ELEVATION

The development of the front and side elevations proceeded much more quickly than the
rear elevation, partly because they were relatively simpler and partly because the library
had to be built first. Our symbolic intentions
were to fit in and contrast with the existing row
of three houses and to represent faces and the
London column. In my original design for the
Solar House, the column was the implicit 'nose'
of a face below a sun altar (1). As mentioned,
Terry thought we would not be able to build so
high and so in December he proposed a lower
mansard roof and nestled the library further
into the kitchen (2). The next stage was my
suggestion that the mansard have a double curve,
or 'Hildebrandtian motif', which could be sur-
mounted by two large London column chimneys, and three lesser column motifs (3). These
larger columns were to have sunburst capitals

5

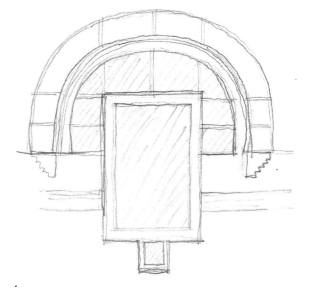

3

4

6

placed above a shaft and a base with a staggered motif, the sign of the earth. This drawing also shows the two faces of Lily and Johnny's rooms breaking through the cornice line. Later I detailed these faces with steel additions which gave them a greater presence and geometrical harmony (4).

My design for the kitchen facade also had symmetrical faces and used a false door to balance the existing one; in the event, this was simplified. This drawing, almost the final synthesis, shows an attempt to centralise the top balcony podium by means of a counter S-curve (5). I ultimately gave up this solution and also changed the topmost balusters (or 'rabbits') to a more abstract grid (6). One can see how the original intentions were carried out in the built solution – the 'faces' transform our neighbour's arch motif; the stucco rustication and the 'rabbits' are continued; the abstract grid is introduced in the faces and balcony to unite with the grids on the other two sides.

1

THE SIDE ELEVATION

The west elevation, facing the setting sun, was given a strong presence which could be read in several ways. At the top of this drawing (1) is a pair of chimneys – London columns with a sunburst at the top and staggered base, the sign in ancient Greece of the earth. To either side are echoes of these columns which were finally dropped because they looked too fussy and replaced by staggered windows which Maggie wanted in order to let in more light. Below this level the curved shape and face further centralise the facade, a concern of mine to be seen in several drawings. My idea was that two contrary visual movements would intersect, some lines converging on the centre, others leading on the diagonal to the edges, so that a dynamic tension would be set up (a baroque formula). This tension is increased by suddenly dropping the 'rabbit' motif – the rabbits are actually sheared in half to indicate their representational or non-structural role. The place where this lands symbolises the floor level of the library.

My sister Penny Jencks, a sculptress, was then asked if she would create personifications of Art and Architecture to set on or beside the two plinths (2). These two figures were to provide a visual culmination to the sweep of the corner S-curves – very important visual points – while semantically they were to represent the tension between art and architecture today. They hold conventional instruments of their trade and turn both to and away from each other to symbolise their perplexed relationship in our society. In the event they were not cast and the plinths still await some symbolic accent.

The axonometric (3) shows how further elements were pulled together. I designed a steel-gridded pediment to take one's eye off the undersized curve of the face and to unite it with the grids I had designed above and below. Like the 'windows on the world', this grid was meant to be so obvious and normal as to disappear from perception. It seems to me that some

2

background ornament is always needed to pull together the foreground ornament, or symbols. A curious foreground shape in this drawing is the oval 'hole' indented in the corner of the roof. Maggie insisted on this to save one branch of a locust tree that now comes across the library balcony (4). I know of only two other examples in which architecture inflects to accept a growing or living tree – one is a gate by Borromini and the other a church by the contemporary Norwegian architect Per Kartvedt. Our own version does afford a pleasant contrast between the organic and built, although it means that in a storm there is a banging on the roof and the next morning too many leaves in

the gutter.

The west facade as built has a haunting presence which is a result not only of the columns and faces, but also of the overall figure. At night the facade looms out like an oversized animal – another rabbit with chimneys for ears, windows for eyes and a central curved snout above a small mouth. The image, which was unintended, is quite apparent in a painting of the facade by Chris Moore reproduced on the cover of *Towards a Symbolic Architecture*. It is, I believe, another example of the way anthropomorphic and animal images arise quite inevitably from architecture with a symmetrical design and pitched roof.

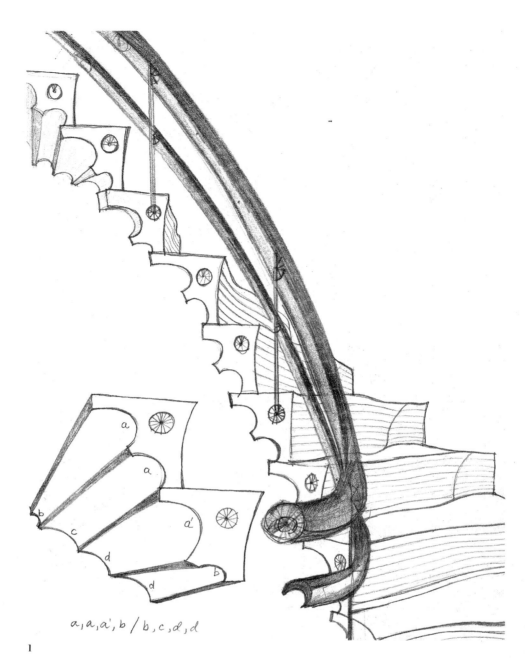

a,a,a',b / b,c,d,d

1

THE SOLAR STAIR

The stairway was conceived as a representation of the sun from the moment we decided it would be a spiral. The connection of such a form and the sun is traditional and was used by Inigo Jones in the stair at the Queen's House in Greenwich, a structure I had always admired. Maggie and I went to study its form, in particular the underneath ribs which had a natural solar flare. What we noticed was that these ribs had a steady beat, a more or less repetitive rhythm. When Terry suggested we could prefabricate different concrete moulds for roughly the same cost, I made some clay models which varied the rhythm and curved the top of the tread. This produced, looking down, an S-curve shape which was more sun-like than a straight line and, looking up, a pulsation of rays even more representational of heat and light than Jones's stairway.

The first models and drawings show a com-plex alternation of shapes – a,a,a',b at the front and b,c,d,d, at the back (1). In effect what are equal shapes at the front became different at the back and vice-versa. This was both visually and logically a neat solution. Also evident in these early sketches is a dark handrail, conceived in black wood, brass or stainless steel, which was to be tied into holes remaining from the fabrication.

The next phase involved the study of systems of cosmic and musical notation to try to find a set of conventions we could use for the rails and ornamental discs. This phase was long and involved and produced many false starts and designs which came to nothing. One of the most interesting of these was called the 'music of the spheres' and equated the rail supports with musical notes, the treble-clef, and other analo-gies taken from astronomy (2). Although such ideas were not taken up directly they did lead to further developments which were incorporated here and outside on the garden stairway where the steel rails and globe supports are intert-wined in a musical way.

Later we consulted Dr McNally, an astro-nomer at the Royal Observatory, on the possi-ble astronomical significance of certain points in the stair and he came up with the following parallels: the first and last sets of two steps could signify the period of the asteroid Eros; the first set of thirteen steps could signify the number of times the sun rotates in a year; the next nineteen steps refer to the Callipic cycle of the moon rotating in its orbit; and the last sixteen refer to Saros, or the repetitions of lunar eclipses (3). All the meanings therefore stay within the orbit of the solar system.

From here it was a short step to deciding on the ornament and meaning of the handrails. Since the three rails could be of different size we decided they should represent the path of the sun, earth and moon as they revolve through space in a spiral manner. Aluminium globes were cast to make these solar metaphors more explicit. The next question was obviously to decide what the flange joints between the con-

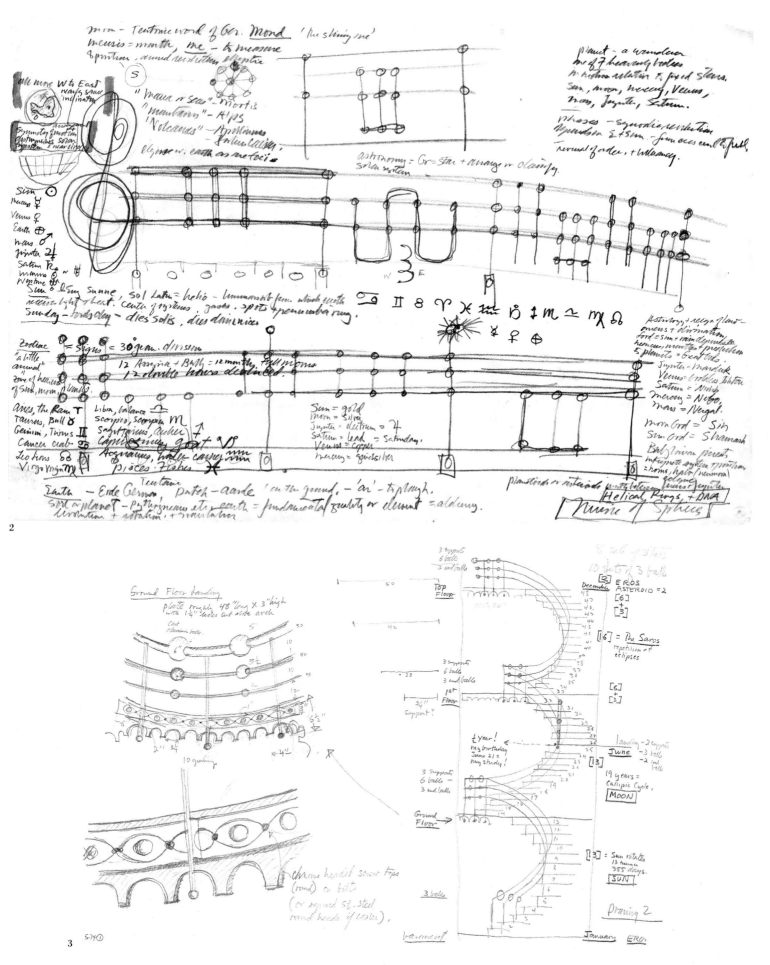

4

crete and steel should represent. Our final choice was the sine curve, a symbol of time and change, which also occurs at the front entrance. The tiny steel balls at the end of each vertical support are clearly asteroids or comets.

The final phase of design concerned the sequence of the steps. Two options were possible for the fifty-two steps (forty-eight plus four) – the year could begin either at the bottom or the top. Since ascension is the natural way one initially reads a stair, we decided that the bottom should be January. I redesigned the signs of the zodiac (4) and surrounded them with whirling planets (zoe = life, diakos = wheel). Ilinca Cantacuzino then oversaw their production as the figures were etched onto mirror discs and placed in the voids of each step. Thus as one walks up the steps, small ornamental signs indicate where one is in the solar year.

While we were designing the visual and symbolic aspects of these stairs, Terry Farrell and David French were working on their structural capacity – the fact that the cylinder of concrete and stair units together formed a good structural shape strong enough to hold up the chimneys on either side of it. We asked them to leave holes wherever possible, both for cross views and so one could see people, or their feet, coming up and down. The results of this collaboration are perhaps the most satisfying in the house, since now the stair acts not only as a structural and symbolic whole, but as a spatial unifier as well. When David Quigley counted the steps and found there were fifty-two, we decided to divide each unit further into seven horizontal notches, resulting in 364 units from bottom to top: almost an exact year.

The final piece of solar and cosmic imagery was Eduardo Paolozzi's *Black Hole* mosaic at the bottom (5). This contrasted entropy (the running down of the universe) with the way up, towards light, heat and hope (6). This opposition, based on Christian iconography and the connotations of climbing and descending, was part of the symbolic programme I wrote for Paolozzi. In the event he produced a colourful black hole that picks up the S-curves of the surrounding units. The colour also changes its quality as one approaches; the predominant blackness slowly reveals many other hues and the surface seems to sparkle and glow. It is a good example of art and architecture mutually enlivening each other.

5

6

THE MOONWELL

The Moonwell is opposite the Solar Stair, directly on axis and connected to it by a green pathway of carpet. Originally we had conceived of including a moon in the kitchen and although its 'rays' remain on the dining room ceiling, it had to be covered up in the end. The lunar idea was then transferred to its present location in a half-moon of space. The way we came to this conclusion was somewhat circular.

In our first design for the Solar House I had imagined an open stairway going up the space that is now occupied by the Moonwell. When we later consulted with Terry he thought of retaining this shaft of space as a way to bring light to a dark part of the house. The idea corresponded with my own and was not dissimilar to the shafts of light which Charles Moore cut into his house in New Haven. My first design for this space, made in December 1978, shows it as a giant London column of mirrors, with light columns to either side of it at the bottom (1). Naturally I used arch forms since these were compatible with the curved top of the London column. It wasn't until we saw this space as the Moonwell that these arches received globe lights and Simon Sturgis added further positive arches above them (2). This drawing shows how the sun and moon rays and the moon's face were incorporated in the window mullions which use Egyptian sun rays as hands coming from the sun god. The top quarter-moon window used in the final design was conceived at this time (December 1981) as was the outline of a face. This idea of man-in-the-moon was finally incorporated in the engraving on the mirror, along with a representation of the Chinese myth of Liu Hai and the three-legged toad (3). This myth concerns immortality and the way the Chinese traditionally projected immortal toads and Taoists – in their mind – onto the moon. John Keswick, Maggie's father, was particularly fond of this myth and had a good collection of these mysterious toads. One can be distinguished along with Liu Hai's face after one has stared at the moon etching for some time. The etching was placed above a wall of mirrors I designed to recall those of the garden conservatories, another example of our attempts to consolidate meanings by transforming similar patterns (4). When one looks up the Moonwell, the eight phases of the moon are visible in the light globes and mirror reflection (5). Since the space is a half-moon, the mirror completes it to give the illusion of a complete circle. And since the 'silvery moon' is the way many people conceive of its colour, we have kept the space light, cool and white.

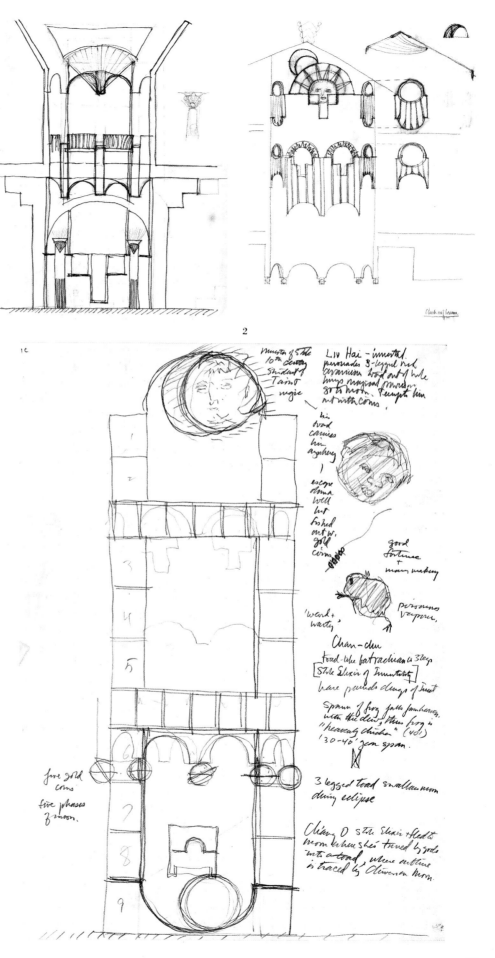

1

2

3

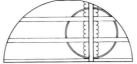

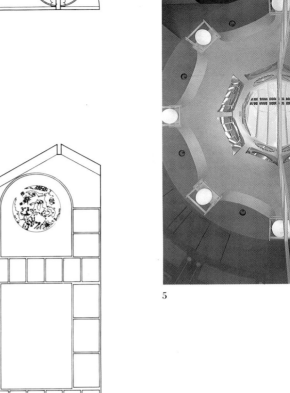

5

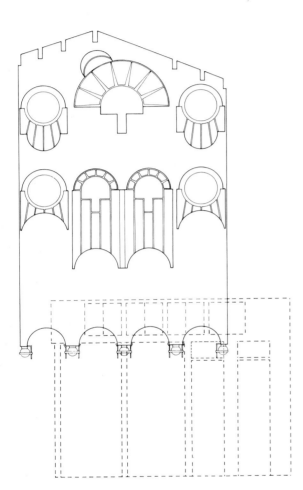

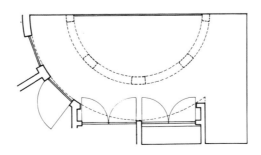

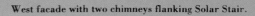

C LAW IS
TIME'S RHYTHM WHICH
RULES SUN & MOON
THE FOUR SEASONS TOO
GIVING HEAT & LIGHT
OVER ALL ARCHITECTURE
EGYPT & CHINA BEC

ELECTIVE AFFINITIES
GOETHE
OVER ALL ARCHITECTURE
EGYPT & CHINA BEGIN

'Windows on the World' lead from the Cosmic Oval into Winter and Spring Rooms. *Above:* The mural by William Stok shows the evolution of the cosmos and cultural time starting with the Egyptians. *Opposite above:* Cosmic Oval 'dome' representing heavens and infinity, and the Cosmic Loo with its postcard frieze and stencilled paronyms of the cosmos.

Spring with its light coloured fireplace designed by Michael Graves, with sculpture of months by Penelope Jencks. *Opposite above*: Sundial Arcade is oriented south and to the garden behind a large mechanical sash window, and view into Egyptian Room showing stylisation of Nile mud and pyramid in ornament (below) and lotus frieze (above). *Opposite below*: View from Winter to Spring – Autumn far right.

Summer Dining Room with its heat and light columns to either side of the Sun Table. *Opposite above:* Summer Room – a wall of mirror doors pulls out. *Opposite below:* The Indian Summer Kitchen with its 'Hindu' storage units.

The Solar Stair with the Black Hole mosaic by Eduardo Paolozzi. *Opposite above:* View through moon windows to the floating image of the moon. *Opposite below:* The Moonwell reflects its half circle and phases of the moon.

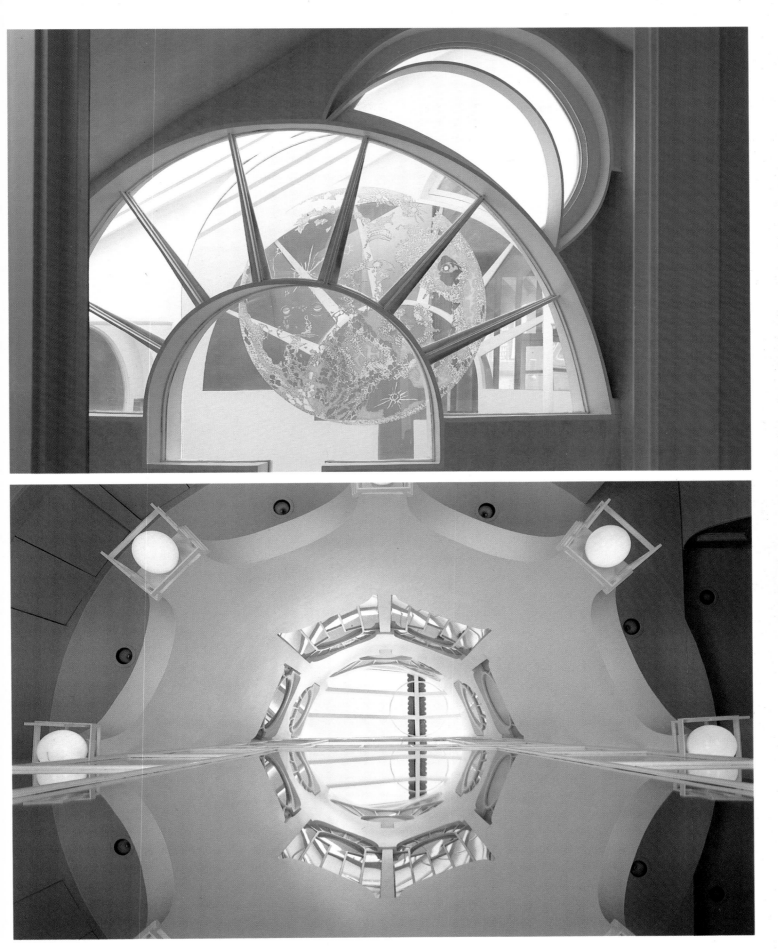

The Architectural Library showing bookcases in the
style of the books they hold. *Opposite above:* Greek
architectural books far left, Roman books centre,
Early Medieval far right. *Opposite below:* Late-
Medieval far left, Renaissance and Mannerism
behind the Slide Skyscraper.

The Foursquare Bedroom with the tetramorph repeated in the furniture, rug, ceiling, ornament and lights. *Opposite*: View from bedroom to bathroom (below), and dressing room (above).

Nan's Room with its stylised owl drawers and window face. *Opposite above:* Lily's Room with some of its stylised water lilies. *Opposite below:* Johnny's Bedroom with its smiling face motif of drawers and window.

View south to the Time Garden and Future Pavilion,
a trompe l'oeil through to the next garden

INTRODUCTION

Terry Farrell

IN NOVEMBER 1978 I RECEIVED A LETTER OUT OF THE blue from Charles Jencks and his wife, Maggie, requesting my involvement in the design and construction of their house. This was followed by a meeting at which I was shown a set of freehand-drawn plans that the Jenckses had done and a set of plans that a building surveyor, Mark Fisher, had drawn up in order to help the Jenckses to realise their ambitions. They had come to me, it was explained, because they had discovered that the process of them having the architectural ideas and a building surveyor effectuating them was not going to work. They needed an architect, and particularly one who could be involved as designer. I was very intrigued by this proposal as I knew, of course, of Jencks's work and I particularly liked the ideas Maggie had for making a home from the building they had bought.

Although from the outset it was made clear to me that the Jenckses, and in particular Charles, would like to have some involvement in the design and development of the house, I have written this article in response to the description set out by Charles Jencks in his book *Towards a Symbolic Architecture* as I feel strongly that this book concentrates primarily on Jencks's own contribution and on the interior decoration and ornamentation of the house to the extent that the Terry Farrell Partnerships' architectural contribution is not clearly and properly recorded. For two-and-a-half years the Jencks house was the major project in my office and one in which I personally was very involved. From the first meeting we introduced new concepts, particularly spatial and planning concepts, which quite changed the direction of the architecture of the house and placed our practice very much in the driving seat in developing the resultant architecture during this period.

I sought a clear dividing line between my architectural ambitions and Jencks's when he came to me about his house. At the outset and in many subsequent letters I established the difference between our roles – that I would be responsible for what I called the shell and that he could be responsible for the follow-on decorative work. This was as much a practical proposition as an architectural one. I knew Jencks could cope perfectly well with the interior decoration and I also knew that when it came to the ideas which were to be applied I would probably not agree with his particular view of classical Post-Modernism. So the essence of our relationship was established as one in which we would part company once the shell of the building was completed.

The idea of the architect being the provider or enabler through the shell design of a house had been preoccupying me quite a bit at this time. I was teaching at the Architectural Association in 1978/79 and had set the students a project entitled 'Learning from Chigwell' after Venturi's Las Vegas project. I set this because our practice was designing two large housing schemes in Warrington New Town where we were completing our design work in a form that would enable the tenants of the local authority houses to have

as much scope as possible within their tenure arrangements to adapt and personalise their homes. Designing homes which take into account personal taste and individual needs for self-expression places the architect in the role of a scriptwriter rather than an actor on stage. At Chigwell, a London suburb, we photographed and recorded with the students the range of add-ons, decorative styles and different expressions of personal taste that had emerged onto the external surfaces of these relatively standard 1930s semi-detached housing. Our drawings for Oakwood anticipate this need for self-expression and in its own way I saw my role with the Jenckses as one in which the client – in this instance well-informed and with an architectural background – was nevertheless unable to produce the shell, had come to me specifically to get it, and had very strong desires to personalise it after my work was over.

In no way did we loan any staff to Jencks to draw up his ideas at this time although after we had completed our two-and-a-half years of work I did agree to lend him staff to help him with his decorative schemes. During this period we produced nearly 1,000 drawings and put in over 6,000 man-hours. There was always one assistant full time on the project. The first was Tom Politovitz (who left this project to be for a short time project architect for our Wood Green factories). He was followed by David Quigley. David for one-and-a-half years made a major contribution to the project; in September 1980 he went on a scholarship to the University of Pennsylvania and was followed by Simon Sturgis who carried on his role as job-architect and again made a substantial contribution. Both David and Simon had other assistants helping them during this period and in particular the contributions of Joe Foges, Simon Hudspith and Neil Porter should be mentioned. The basis of our appointment was for the full RIBA architectural services for which we received the full fees for conversion work. I devised a particularly complex and ambitious contractual approach whereby a main contractor produced a series of serial tenders and had a host of smaller sub-contractors who were directed on a day-to-day basis almost on an artist and tradesman's level. This was in order that the design could develop in stages so that when the Jenckses returned from their lengthy trips away from London we could re-assess the position, renew their involvement and agree the next stage of construction work. It wasn't the most economical way to proceed but it was certainly the most flexible, and interestingly was one that leaned rather heavily on the contractual know-how of fast-track programming that I had developed in the old Farrell/Grimshaw factory and industrial building sphere.

It is interesting to look at many of the projects that led up to the kind of thing I was doing by adding on at the Jencks house. Adding on to London terrace housing in order to extend the spatial volume of the house or to add modern amenities was the basis of many early projects. We have quite a different attitude today to

Below: Ground level (west half of house), May 1980.
Inset: Ground plan, December 1978.

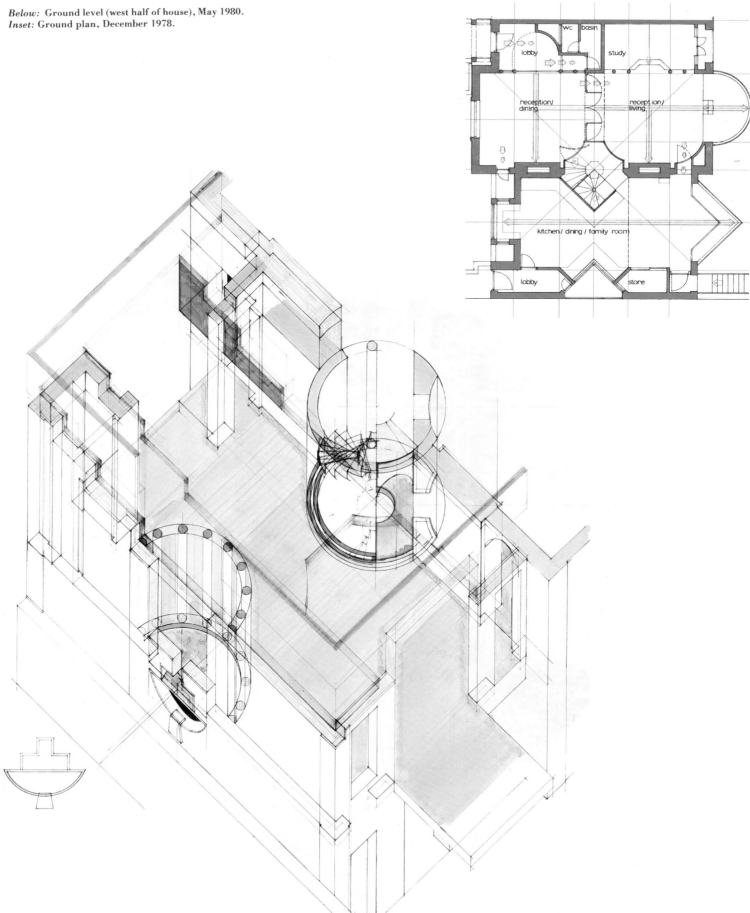

Below: Ground level (east half of house), May 1980.
Inset: Ground plan, May 1979.

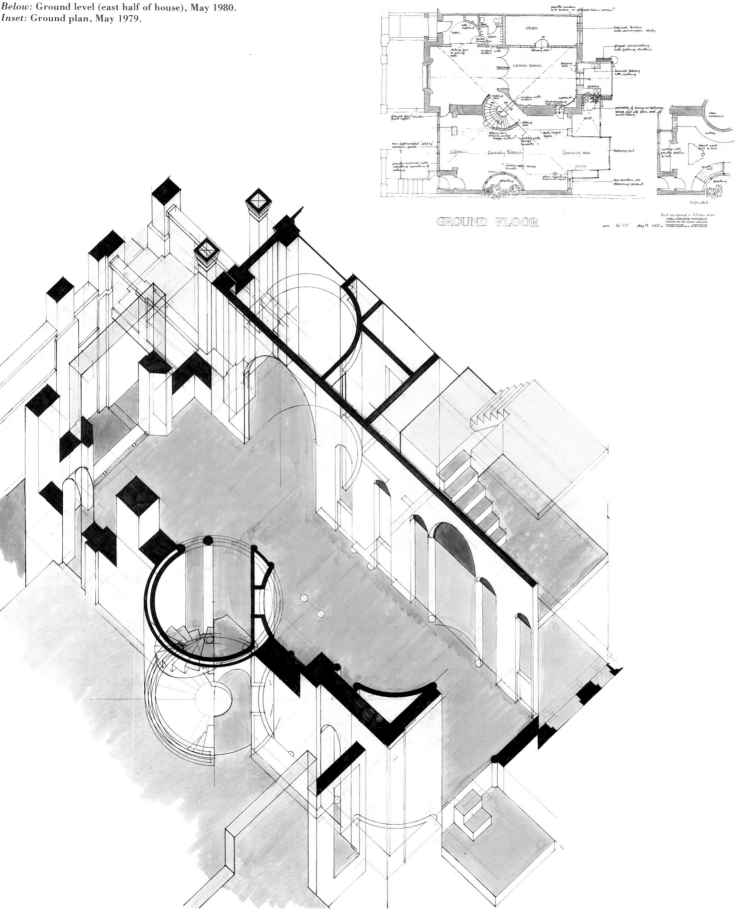

GROUND FLOOR

the front and back of houses: previous generations did not value views over gardens or southern orientation or lack of noise intrusion from the street and house plans were therefore standardised and not varied according to their orientation or view. Much of the conversion work I have done on private house design and terraced house rehabilitation in London has therefore begun with reassessing the standard house types' disregard of aspects. My very first project, for a student hostel, (1965–68) involved the addition of a service tower to free existing staircases to become bedrooms and to add on all the new service elements of bathrooms and toilets. At Porchester Square where eight large terraced houses were converted into eighty apartments, all the existing finer rooms of these houses looked out over the newly created square which the Victorian developer had laid out to help sell the houses. But as the square is on the north side, I added a building at the rear, butting right up against the old back wall, to make the house three rooms deep from front to back. The new rear rooms then became the living rooms and the old fine rooms the bedrooms, so that the living rooms could look out into a newly created private garden on the south side. By juggling the floor-levels we were also able to have quite a degree of spatial interlocking between the new add-on building and the existing one.

The Smith house in Islington in 1975 completely reversed the existing plan in much the same way as we did at the Jencks house by placing the staircase (again circular) towards the front of the house and opening up the whole width of the rear of the house, which had previously been stair and kitchen, for living accommodation. In 1979–80 in Covent Garden, eight apartments were created from three existing historic houses. Leaving the front untouched we created a rear addition of lift and service units that extended no more than one metre because of space constrictions at the rear. By re-using half-landings in the existing staircase we were able to reorientate completely the circulation and room configuration for the entire building. Finally, in the Rothschild house in St John's Wood in 1981–82, the add-on was at the front of the house in that the little studio was inbalanced on its front elevation with a minor annexe to one side of the front door. The facade was adjusted in not too different a manner to the much larger annexe added to the Jencks house. It is probably one of the basic drives behind rehabilitation work that the existing resource is plundered, recycled and exploited for its maximum character and space potential. My own house, which I began in 1974, is now fondly referred to by the family as 'The Tardis' – a science fiction story spacecraft which is perceived from the outside as a police telephone box but from the inside as an enormous spaceship. The three-bedroom semi-detached house was eventually made into a five-storey multi-roomed house and by exploiting the lowest, subterranean areas and the roof-top areas, space has been added to adjacent rooms to make more space and more character.

A central preoccupation of the first Post-Modernist spatial organisations is a move towards greater introversion and complexity. Modernist space is by comparison universal (each can suit another use), entropic (limitless, non-hierarchical, spatially unconstrained) and generally suffers, as Denys Lasdun once observed, from agoraphobia. Post-Modern space, as with most things Post-Modern, suffers from trying too hard to be the opposite and so tends to be over-compartmented and so highly organised in elemental terms that in the end it can suffer from claustrophobia. The desire endlessly to work up an abundance of small-scale incidents extends to the ever-minute layering of symbolism, story-telling decoration and so on. It is quite clear in the end, however, that the Post-Modern space is not a backdrop space – it is not a space in which the occupant is free to express whatever he likes, whenever he likes, as Foster and Rogers see their offices and factories. The Post-Modern space is highly particular – each part is allocated its role and its character is set and its opportunities explored by the designer rather than the occupant. In the Jencks house, the 'shell' is therefore itself a series of set pieces, resolved to a certain point of concept and detail onto which is layered the personal decorative work of the owners which in itself has its own existence and story to tell.

Before I proceed to report on the specific elements of our design work on the Jencks house, I think a general note about the reasons for wanting to sort out who did what should be stated. For the first year or two I was referred to as the architect by the Jenckses and all who dealt with the house, but at the time of handing on the baton to Jencks I recognised that there would have to be some recording of the credit and some adjustment of the concept that I had had the major role. I proposed to Jencks therefore, and we agreed, that the credits should ultimately be shared: Farrell and Jencks. With a client as architecturally informed as Jencks, it is obvious that an architect entering into an appointment must recognise that the client will make through his briefing, criticism and constructive sketching and observations, a major contribution. What then is conceptual briefing and what architecting? What the historian-critic wishing to make a mark on the architectural scene has to contribute is quite different from architecture as a practised art; likewise, what the architect through his experience, skill and craftsmanship produces is quite different from the talents brought to bear by the informed client. My comments in this article are motivated entirely in order to try to produce an objective historical record of the design of a house that is, I believe, of some importance. I am grateful to the publishers for agreeing to let me have this space as I feel particularly strongly that there should be a record, not only for historical purposes but also for the credit of the job architects and their assistants from this practice who will testify to the work they did full time for two-and-a-half years.

All models, including inside covers, by Terry Farrell Partnership.

Opposite: Terry Farrell Partnership models of August 1980 showing construction of annexe.

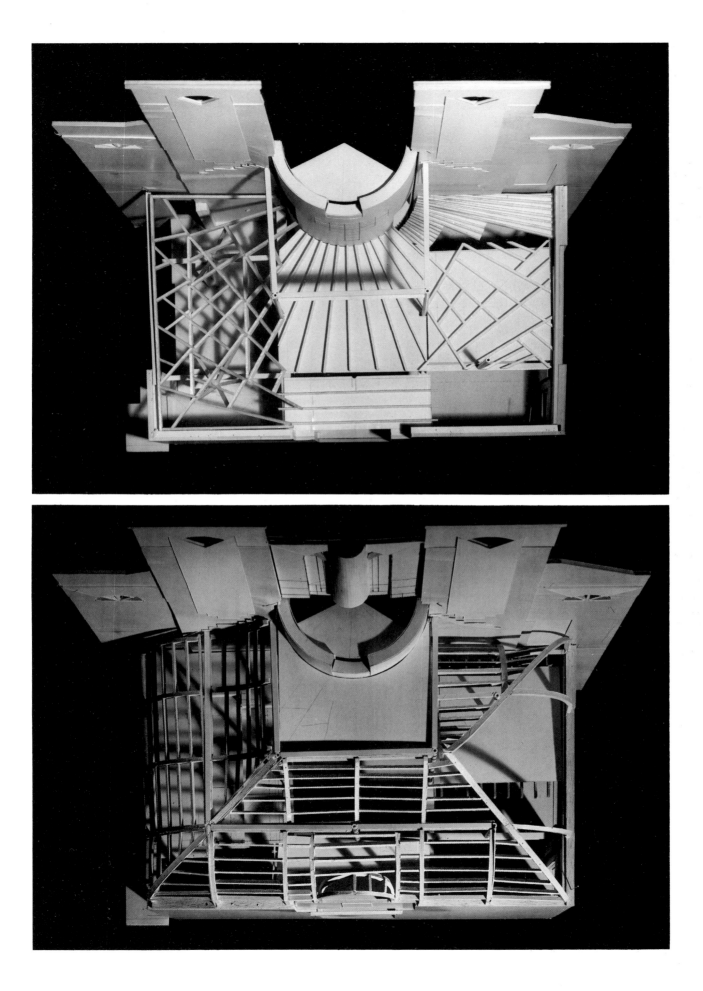

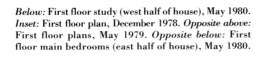

Below: First floor study (west half of house), May 1980. *Inset:* First floor plan, December 1978. *Opposite above:* First floor plans, May 1979. *Opposite below:* First floor main bedrooms (east half of house), May 1980.

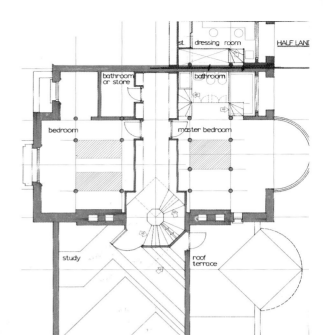

dressing room

HALF LAND

bathroom or store

bathroom

bedroom

master bedroom

study

roof terrace

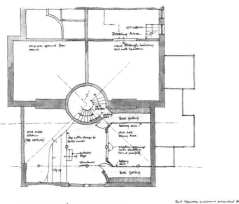

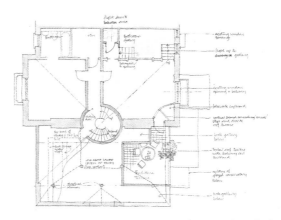

STAGE 1:
DESIGNING THE ADD-ONS

The Jenckses' plan as placed before me in November 1978 contained a lot of architectural ambitions, most of which I considered to be either impractical or, if practical, either difficult to get planning permission for or uneconomical. I saw these plans not as plans as such but as a method of drawing out the client's brief. This is a starting point I have often received from well-informed clients (for example, in my very first job on a student hostel in Sussex Gardens) and is one which can often articulate a brief better than the written word.

I addressed myself in the first instance to the problems of the intended add-ons; new conservatories at the rear and an extra storey or two to the side annexe. The side annexe proposals in particular worried me because they would quite clearly not get planning consent because of their bulk and I also did not believe that the existing small building could carry that amount of extra structure. The rear conservatories were seen at that time as three individual buildings stuck onto the back. I believed that they did not develop the full spatial potential of the internal rooms and also that a simpler solution was possible using only two conservatories in the centre of the house which would extend the two main central bays and possibly interlink spatially at the lower main floor levels.

The 'compressed annexe' concept
At a meeting only a few weeks after we were commissioned, I presented in very rough sketch form the essence of my ideas to lower the extra studio floor on the annexe and compress it over the top of the annexe so that it would read more as a large roof over the existing annexe than as an extra floor. The compression of this roof upon the lower floors meant that the ceiling and roof of the ground floor had to be removed completely. This provided an opportunity to create an interrelationship between the studio and its underside – a dining and kitchen space – and right from the outset I suggested that if, in order to achieve this spatial compression, the studio library had a stepped profile, then this would release opportunities for a varied ceiling form on the underside in the kitchen and dining room. In addition, the removal of the floor/ceiling provided an opportunity for visual links between these spaces. I was also particularly keen that as the ceiling level on the ground floor area was to be lowered there should still be a higher ceiling over the dining table. My sketches therefore proposed a centrally placed dining area at the rear garden side, with side windows at a higher level to look down into this space from the studio library. The windows in the studio library were right from this early stage proposed as being tiny windows inserted between an extended version of the existing stone balustrading so that from the outside there did not appear to be an extra floor at all and from the inside one had a view through a fretwork of the balusters which were always humorously referred to as the 'Rabbits' because that's what they looked like from the inside of the room.

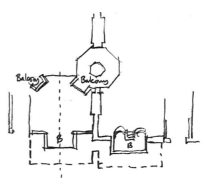

Left: The first sketch of the compressed annexe concept. *Right:* The paired interlocking conservatories.

The 'paired interlocking conservatories' concept
Rather than simply adding on vertical shafts of glass conservatories at the back, at this same meeting I also proposed that the conservatories be seen not so much as extensions to each of the rooms of the house – one on top of the other and in an unlinked manner like stacked bay windows – but instead be concentrated at the bottom and in the centre of the house. I proposed that the two conservatories should have a spatial link between each other and a link by views between the ground floor and the lower ground floor so that the main rooms of the house overlooking the garden would be spatially more dynamic. In the first sketches this scheme showed a considerable interlinking of these spaces; as built this spatial interest is maintained with the exception that the main living-room space at the garden side does not link up spatially with the dining-room conservatory. However, I established that the dining-room conservatory should be double-height with the dining space itself forming a balcony overlooking the garden floor part of the conservatory and that at the garden level there should be a horizontal link between both conservatories so that there would be a single space across the back of the house at garden level. This concept was retained right through the project and is now built.

It was rather strange that a lot of what I would call the architectural issues were not part of our discussions with the client. From the very beginning, the intermittent discussions we had when Jencks was in this country were about his search for a symbolic decorative language, an issue he felt very strongly about but which tended to dominate discussions so that the actual work we were getting on with of architecting was given less discussion time. I suppose this was inevitable in that a lot of what we were doing was so linked to what was essential and practical that there were always good reasons why a plan form or a space or a shape was emerging the way it was. The real architectural discussions we had resulted in presentations of ideas to the client such as the central staircase, the compressed annexe, the complex roof spaces and the interlocking volumes. These were all generally seen as strong ideas that were accepted relatively quickly without too much discussion.

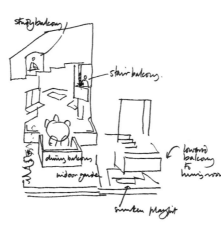
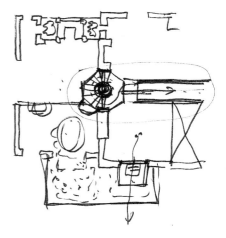

Left: The interlocking of annexe and conservatory spaces. *Right:* The first sketch of the centrally placed stair.

THE CENTRAL STAIRCASE

The only dramatic idea that stood out clearly from Jencks's plan of 1978 was for a staircase opening up from one side of the main room in the form of the letters 'K' and 'C' interlocked to reflect the owners' initials. I felt that there were difficulties of scale and spatial resolution here and the circulation throughout the house remained unresolved for a month or two into our working on the project. The Jenckses had indicated that they were flexible on the position of the stair in the house – it could move to the centre or the edges but it was generally agreed that its present position at the back of the house was unacceptable because it occupied valuable room space on the south side overlooking the garden. The idea of placing the stair in the absolute centre, between the chimneys, emerged in the design session with Politowitz, Quigley and I and was immediately recognised as having great clarity and strength as this position would help us structure the entire scheme for the house, which is how it turned out.

With the stair placed in the centre, the spine wall on which it sits and the structural problems of the continuity of the old party wall between the chimneys required resolution. With David French, an ingenious shaft design was resolved which built a drum from the basement upwards demolishing only a few courses at a time above the drum so that at all times the restraint was continuous between the chimneys. The drum shape in itself was a more than adequate replacement for the wall between the chimneys. What made the structural scheme of things somewhat more complex was that we also decided to build the precast concrete steps for the stair into the cylinder, integrating them into the brickwork so that stair and stair treads were built as one. It was a slow process and it took several weeks to get from the basement to the top of the house. Although the drum itself in its larger form does not continue beyond the roof of the annexe, the brickwork was removed on all storeys for the full height of the house. As the central stairway divided the house clearly into two on either side of the original party wall (one side being the annexe, the other the original house), it was a short step then to make it a foursquare plan by halving each of the two elements again. My desire for a much more dynamic spatial complexity was to be realised through the stair being treated as a vertical shaft which opened into the rooms as it proceeded up the house and, indeed, all rooms open onto the stair and most have windows into and out of this main staircase. One particularly beneficial result of this central placement of the stair is that it replaced a considerable amount of wall area and occurs at what would otherwise have been a rather dead part of the entire plan. In effect it was possible to make all the rooms served by the stair larger than they might otherwise have been and it also saved space by reducing the necessity of corridor runs.

The Solar Staircase

We were now looking at a house plan which had in every way radically moved on from the Mark Fisher plan we first saw. At this time we were

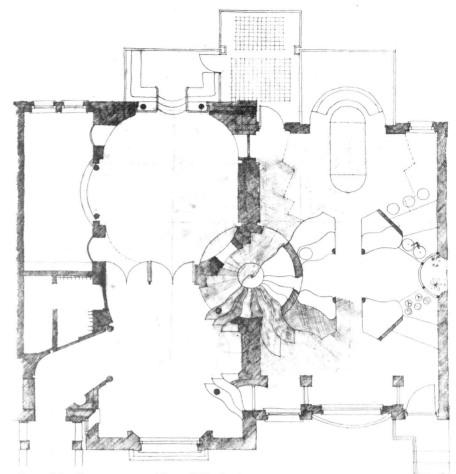

Above: Solar Geometry, ground floor, 1980, showing maximum influence of radial geometry. *Below:* Solar Geometry, first floor plan.

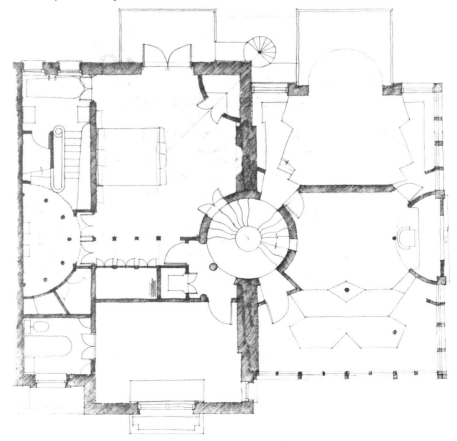

Right: Annexe roof section, March 1979. *Below:* Annexe roof, May 1980. *Opposite above:* Main roof, May 1980, with main roof spaces, plan and section, June 1979 (*inset*). *Opposite below:* Moonwell studies, June 1979.

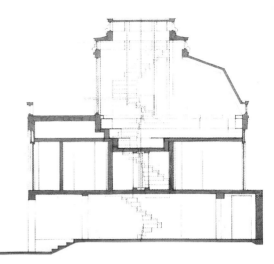

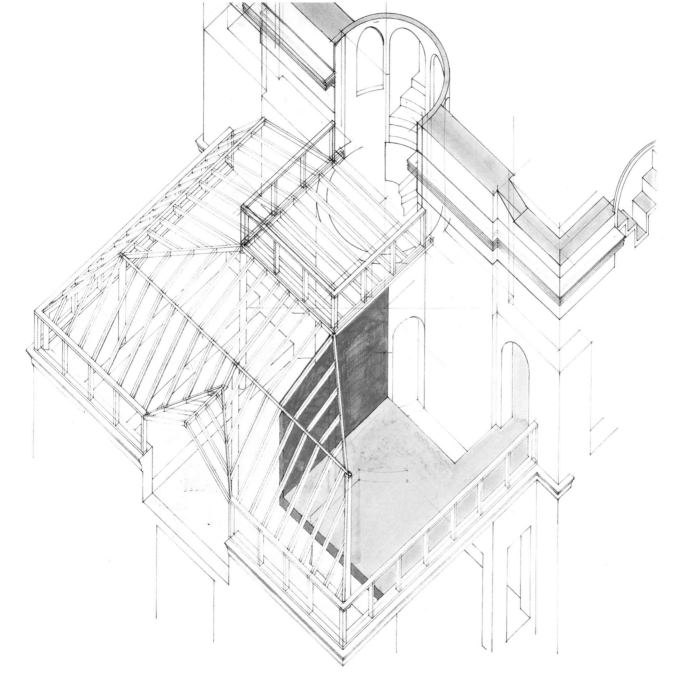

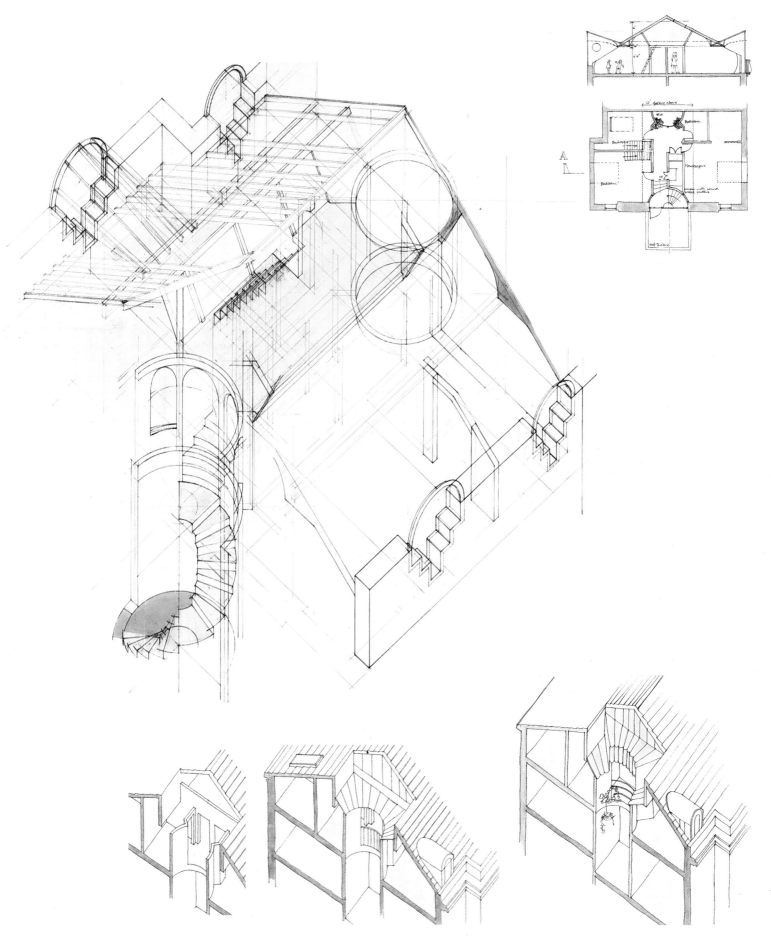

working with Ralph Lebens on various passive solar energy schemes and we developed with him a scheme for the Jencks house in which the conservatories were to be used as a heat trap in the winter. Built into the base of the main circular staircase is a honeycomb of heavy-weight bricks to absorb heat ducted from the top of the conservatories so that the base of the stair would be a warm heat sump from which heat would move up the staircase and through open doors into all of the house. This was all built but the detailed design of the top of the conservatories as it was eventually effectuated prevented the full realisation of the scheme. However, the presence of this solar idea led to the symbolic theme for the house.

The staircase itself was initially a square plan form set at a 45° angle to the rest of the house. When it rose above annexe level it came within the house, into another square-form stair which did not project beyond the party wall. Gradually the design of the stair became octagonal and eventually circular.

The centrality of the stair, its circular form and its solar role soon established an idea in the back of everyone's mind in our office that this was a solar motif, a symbol for the sun. The development of all the symbolism in the house was built upon this single idea, although we did not realise the potency of this idea at the time and were anxiously searching, at the client's behest, for other avenues of symbolic meaning. In this regard, the client was becoming increasingly anxious as his eventual need to develop a decorative language would rely heavily upon what clues the architectural organisation would give him. In the end, the geometrical discipline of the plan was all the assistance one needed to have a range of symbolic themes and indeed I have often found that it is possible to read into strong plan forms a whole host of interpretations according to the predilections of the observer.

The stair tread design was a particular design contribution of Charles Jencks who, inspired by a trip to the Queen's House in Greenwich, wanted a stair tread with a highly sculptured form on the under side as well as a sweeping plan form. The reasons for the stair tread becoming a concern for the client at this early stage was because it was virtually the first element in the shell stage of work where the final visual decorative form would be dictated by the process of precast construction work. In other words, it was not something that could be 'decorated' afterwards. The stair tread was therefore the first interchange we had with Jencks on decorative design and it made me realise that the scope for two designers at a decorative stage was not at all great and that the shell policy I had proposed and adopted was certainly the wisest course to have taken. Nevertheless, I believe that the design of the stair treads was one of the most successful dialogues we had on detailed decorative design, probably because it did lean heavily upon constructional know-how. This was not the case with a lot of the add-ons of trellis work, keystones, etc. at the rear and in parts of the interior which, when they became completely non-constructional and could be freely applied, showed the great disparity between Jencks's preoccupation and ours.

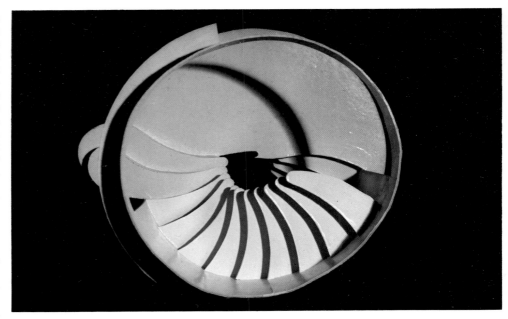

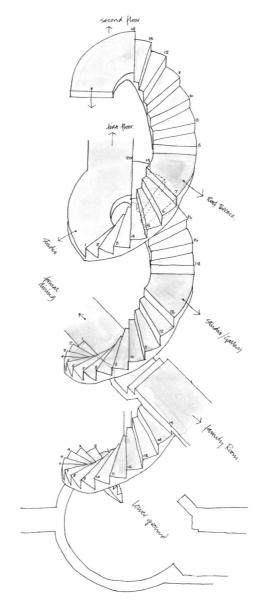

The stair treads, Solar Stair, July 1979.   Study model of Solar Stair, August 1980.

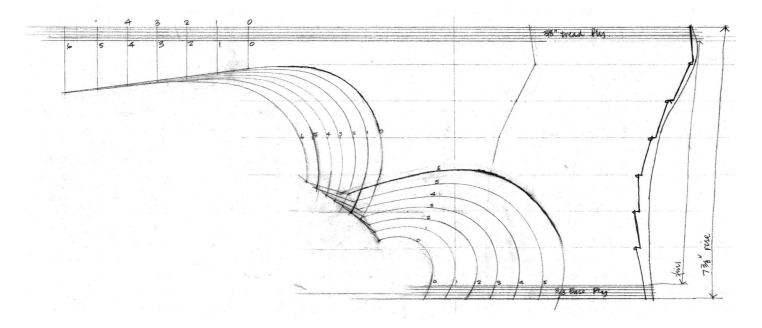

Above: Construction drawing of single pre-cast tread,
July 1979. *Below:* The walls of the cylinder forming
the Solar Stair unwound flat, July 1979.

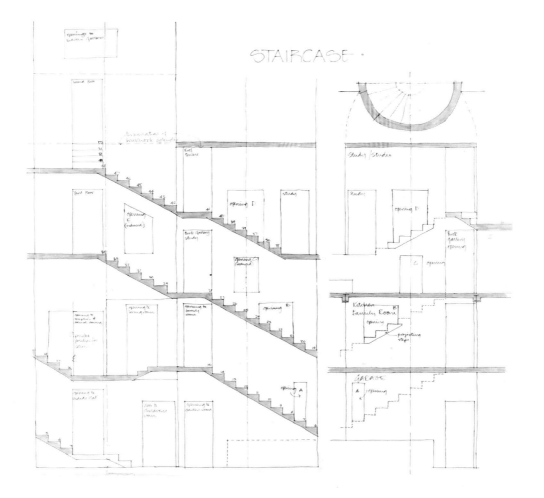

Below: Gable end, basement, May 1980. *Inset:* Gable
elevation, May 1979.

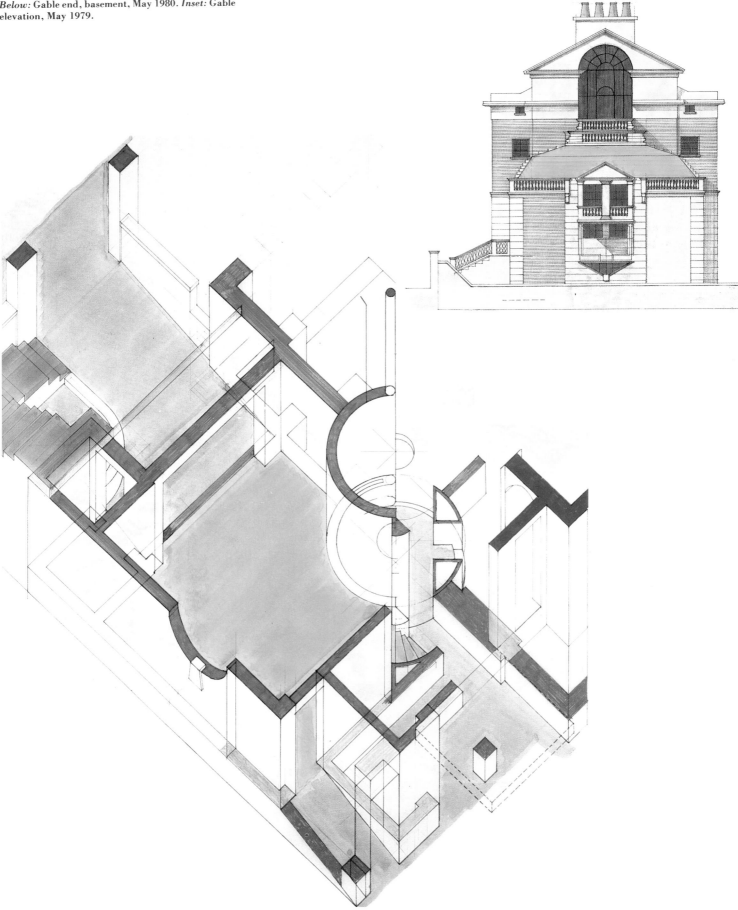

THE MOONWELL

The Moonwell design developed when we were further into the project at a time when the Jenckses were away. Having focused the circulation in the centre of the house, we had been worried for some time that the windows were only round three sides and there was one quite dark area of the plan against the party wall of the adjoining property. This dark area was particularly disadvantageous to the first and second floors. When we developed the Moonwell idea we had already planned out most of the bedroom floors in broad principle and the idea of a lightwell became possible during construction, after we had investigated the roof construction adjoining the party wall. I was particularly excited about the idea of this lightshaft being semi-circular in form with a mirror on the party wall to reflect the borrowed light coming down the lightshaft. At the same time it would be a pale reflection of the central stairwell which by comparison gained direct sunlight. By this time the central stair had become the Sun Stair and almost from the outset this semi-circular lightshaft was called the Moon-

well. As it was so late into the scheme of things when we presented the Moonwell design to the Jenckses it was at first resisted, particularly by Charles, as it required a bit of reorganisation of some ideas already agreed, particularly on the main bedroom floor. However, we adopted it completely in all our drawings from then on and it gradually became accepted as a *fait accompli*. A particular delight of the Moonwell is that it extended the dynamics of the spatial complexity into an area of the house which until this point had been spatially rather static. Indeed, I have often felt when designing interiors that use of borrowed light and mirror can add considerably to the spatial dynamic. Both the Sun Stair and the Moonwell produced circulation areas in the top part of the house lit by daylight although placed centrally, together with an interrelation of rooms which gave a closer family feeling. The circulation routes were the hub of the house in terms of lighting, spatial organisation and movement and reflect something I have always felt strongly about, namely that circulation is a structure and a form in its own right and its celebration even in the family house (or perhaps particularly in the family house) is the essence of the architectural solution.

Below and opposite: The emergence of a detailed design for the Moonwell, January 1981. Our first idea was to construct a dressing table in the form of a miniature of the gable wall at the bottom of the Moonwell.

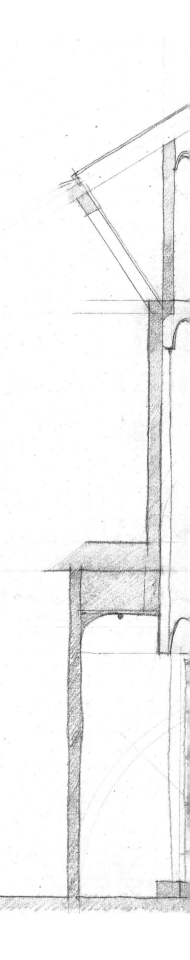

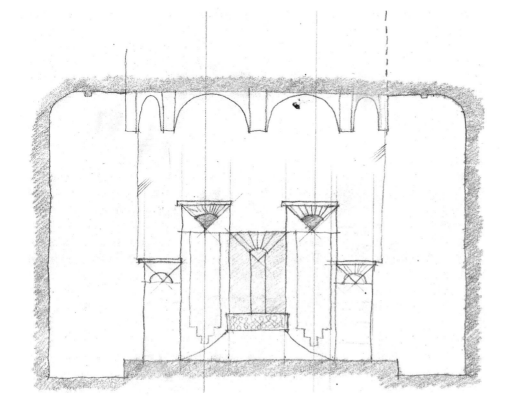

THE TOP FLOOR

With the circulation and the add-ons resolved we could now turn our attention to the individual rooms. We began with the roof, for although this was low in the clients' priorities, it was a very high priority in constructional terms as, logically, the construction work should begin at this level. The roof scheme was therefore developed fairly rapidly and was installed very much to the design of our office (particularly David Quigley) as we had virtually no brief other than that two bedrooms were needed for the children and one for the Nanny with its own bathroom.

I had on several small house conversions over the years and indeed in my own house, with my own children, developed the idea of galleries and cute spaces within roof voids. There is something particularly appealing in designing cute spaces for children: it is something I suppose that one would always like to do for oneself but with the added dimension that children delight in spatial exploration more than adults. A gallery was therefore planned in the centre of the pitch of the roof accessed by means of little stairs from the children's bedrooms and with views into the top of the Moonwell and the Solar Stair on each side. The gallery is supported on a series of central beams which sit like see-saws on a central column. These beams form columns supporting the roof, and indeed can be seen exposed in the Nanny's room where they give a form to the roof. The colonnade of columns that forms the central spine of the see-saws also proceeds down the house and this became a strong determining factor in the plan of the first floor bedroom below, where a colonnade of 4"x4" prime timber posts are exposed. I should mention here that David Quigley was initially trained as a carpenter and his work on site in designing and setting out the complex carpentry with the workmen for the roof and later the curved annexe roof and floor showed a great deal of ingenuity and skill.

The Jenckses wanted particularly large windows in these second floor bedrooms and Charles had indicated his Jencksiana barrel-top windows as being what he would like to see incorporated. The structural detailing of these huge windows proceeded immediately with a great deal of experimentation on site as to how they could be formed. The resultant rooms are well-lit and spatially generous and do not feel at all like left-over attic spaces.

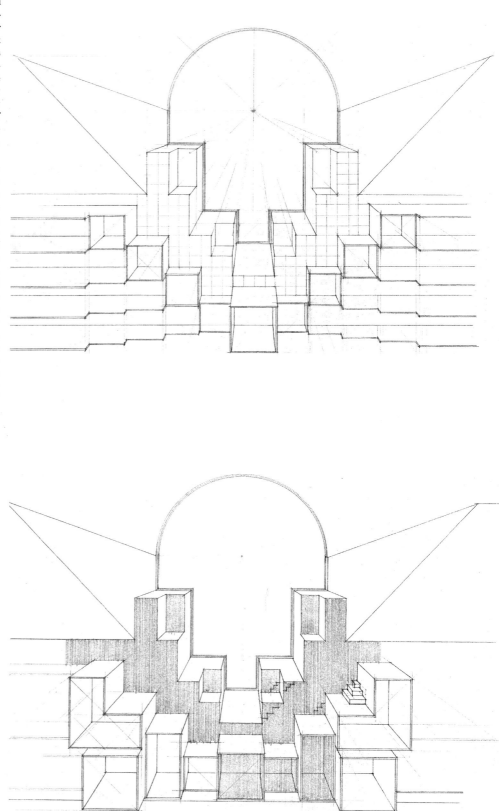

Right: Main room, dormer windows internal treatment, August 1980.

Opposite above: Main roof construction, August 1979. *Opposite below:* Details of main roof construction, December 1979.

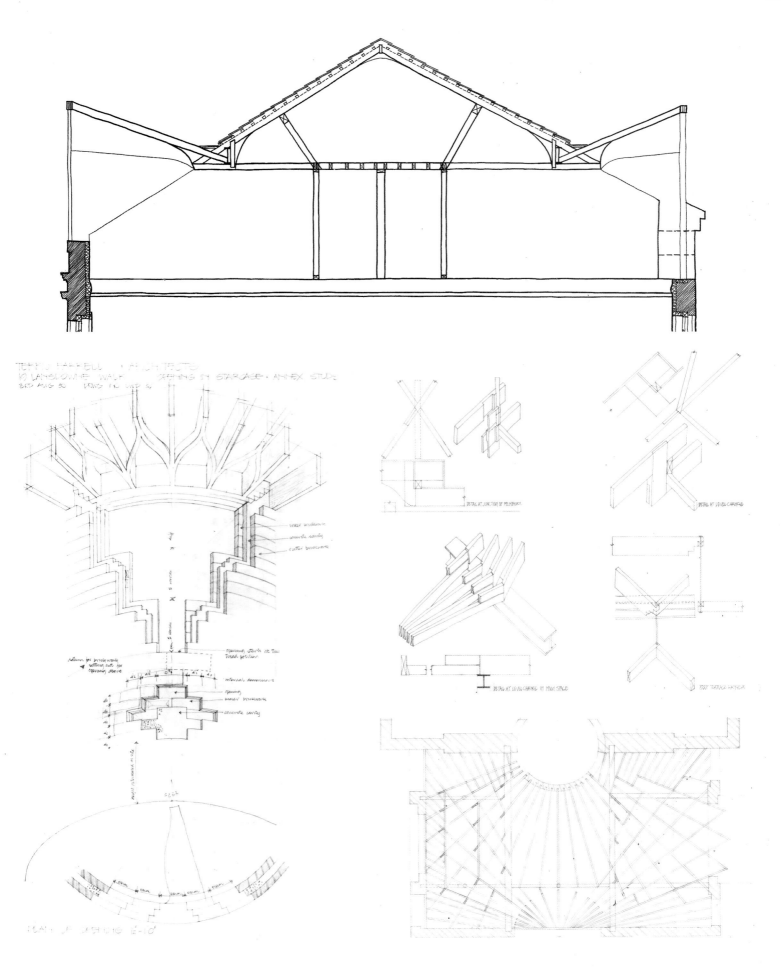

THE FIRST FLOOR
(bedroom and study)

This was always the most difficult floor to resolve. The study beneath the inclined roof with its sunken floor in the centre was always clearly an exciting space. We had initially designed a Mansard roof in order to enclose the maximum volume in straight flat surfaces; Charles Jencks's contribution was to suggest that it be curved, an idea which was developed with some fairly tricky carpentry and lead work detailing by David Quigley. The idea of the flat roof terrace on top of this annexe had existed right from the outset, as had the idea of the central window overlooking the neighbours' garden which had always been a subject of some negotiation with them.

The area that proved the most difficult to resolve was the relationship of the study to the terrace. There was a large tree which overhung the rear of the terrace and we were pleased with the way we adjusted the roof form to fit around it. The way the roof opened around the terrace and met the rear wall was a result of seemingly endless to-and-fro design work between all parties.

The window from the main staircase into the study exposes the layers of construction of the staircase cylinder. The brick drum was constructed from two leaves of brickwork with poured reinforced concrete (into which the pre-cast stair treads were set) in the gap between. This study window unpeels the three layers and the ceiling picks up this exposed structure. As this roof and ceiling and the floor below it to the dining room were the only really new floors in the house, we had the opportunity here to pick up the sun theme by exploring a radial geometry from the central core. The radial construction, like the roof construction, was made possible by complex carpentry detailing and construction, again supervised and detailed on site by David Quigley. The main curved roof elements are plywood, the lower beams are solid timber construction.

The design of the main bedroom began by trying to resolve the void left by the removal of the old stair. I had always wanted to retain some part of this staircase as a reminder of the old plan form; on this floor the stair down gives another half level between ground and first floor for the bathroom, while the stair up enabled us to tuck in a small dressing-room gallery for Charles Jencks. Each of these two half-level spaces looks into the main bedroom through little windows and the stair treads themselves have led to ingenious storage solutions. A lot of the detailing for the bathroom was completed before Charles Jencks began the decoration and the main spatial structure of the bedroom was there as well. In particular, I had resolved the rather oddly shaped room with the curved section biting into it at the central staircase by planning an answering curved dressing area on the other side of the main fireplace. This focused the room on the bed and transformed it from an irregular space into one with a clear cross-axiality. As a result, the rather unstructured windows and views through and from the room play a lesser role in its total perception.

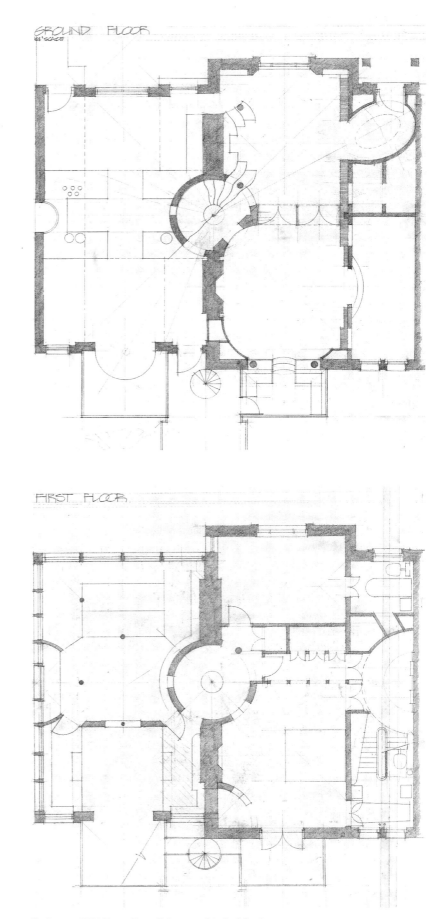

By August 1980 Terry Farrell Partnership had finalised the main floor plans.

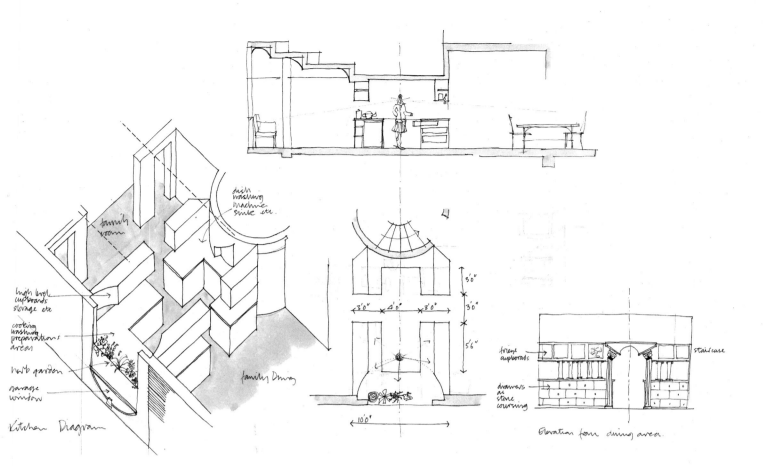

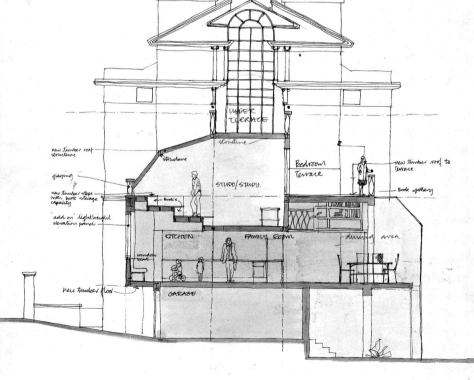

Above: The compressed annexe dictated from the outset the form of the kitchen and dining area below, August 1979.

Left: Section showing the compressed annexe and its interrelationship between ground and first floors as built, August 1979.

We spent a very considerable amount of time on ideas for the colonnade made from the timber supports to the see-saw on the roof; in the end most of these ideas were not built. The Moonwell lights the far end of the bedroom circulation area and provides a linking lobby between bathrooms, dressing room, Maggie's own study bedroom and the main bedroom. Although it presented considerable difficulties in planning terms, once resolved this very active spatial scenario provided an extraordinarily stimulating main bedroom arrangement. Some solutions in architecture come instantly; others only as the result of grinding away! Charles Jencks's decorations in the bedroom area have I feel been particularly successful as they work well with the geometry and spatial framework in which they have been set.

THE GROUND FLOOR:
Final choice of symbolism

The Jenckses had always been fairly clear of their basic spatial requirements for this floor as the existing plan seemed to lend itself so obviously to being divided between living room and dining/kitchen. The central placement of the staircase meant that the stair had to be passed through to get from one half of the house to the other and so fairly early on we introduced link connections at the ends of the gable wall so there would be other routes through. It was while regarding this room and its plan structure that I conceived of the symbolic theme for the house which was then to be maintained through the rest of the development of the scheme.

As mentioned earlier, Charles Jencks had always wanted a theme for the house. When he first came to us a lot of the theme work was based on the names and characters of his family. At a later stage, because there were so many external terraces, it was intended that the house should be known as the 'Terraced House' – Jencks's pun on the London house type and the terraces themselves. However, one day when planning the ground floor with the Jenckses, Charles reiterated his brief that he wanted a design theme based upon a symbolic intention. Until that time we had often referred to the central staircase as the 'Sun', both because of its passive solar heating potential and because it sat centrally within the house plan. It then occurred to me that because of their orientation, the four zones of the house on the ground floor could each be allocated one of the four seasons around the sun. The area where the door and entrance area was I then proposed as a winter room as this was on the north and east of the house and got the least amount of sunlight. The spring room, following logically in a clockwise direction, would be the room that got east and south sunlight and the summer room, the dining room, would get maximum sunshine from its south and west orientation while its double-height conservatory area, top lighting from the studio and central roof light meant that it would be by far the best lit room on the ground floor. Finally, the autumn room would logically be the room where the harvest, the food, was prepared and stored in the kitchen and kitchen storage area.

From the moment of my suggesting the seasons as the basic theme for the house it was picked up and adopted, although I have no doubt that without the client's continuous pursuit of a thematic base we would not have struggled so hard to find the eventual solution. It is often the role of the client to urge the architect on to exercise his imagination; the client's tastes and lifestyle often extend the architect's thinking in directions he would not originally have taken. Although Jencks was driving us to find thematic solutions, I am quite clear in my mind that just as with the spatial formation and plan structure, the eventual symbolism was founded upon the very connections we made, on the essentially architectural process of developing a plan for a house. A good client makes architecture possible and to separate the client's brief and intent from architecture in these cir-

cumstances is difficult, but in the end there *is* a division between being the client and being the architect, between clienting and architecting. All clients perceive many ideas as having been their own and most architects tactfully don't contradict their clients as in the end their client

is not going to claim that he was also the architect. In the case of the Jencks house, any historic reporting of the process of design obviously has to be more carefully appraised.

The final built form of the entrance rooms on the ground floor – the winter and spring rooms

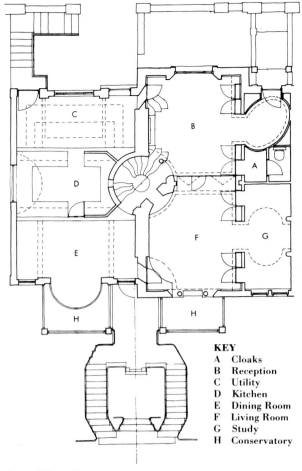

Ground Floor Plan

First Floor Plan

KEY
A Cloaks
B Reception
C Utility
D Kitchen
E Dining Room
F Living Room
G Study
H Conservatory

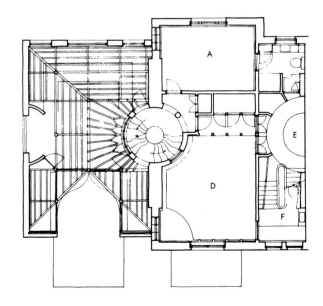

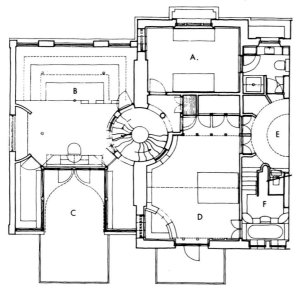

KEY
A Guest Bedroom
B Study
C Terrace
D Master Bedroom
E Dressing
F Bathroom

First Floor Plan

Second Floor Plan

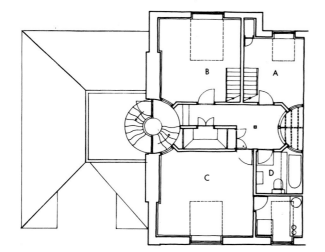

The floor plans on completion as drawn specially for the Architectural Monograph *Terry Farrell*, published by Academy Editions in 1984, pages 52-55. This contains the only joint statement by Farrell and Jencks on their collaboration.

KEY
A Girl's Bedroom
B Boy's Bedroom
C Nanny's Rooms
D Bathroom

– was not the result of a great deal of architectural input by ourselves. Our major contributions therefore focused on the intrusion of the circular staircase and the addition of the conservatory at the rear. The suggestion of lowering the floors of the conservatory was, I believe, made by Maggie Jencks so that any seating in this area would not intrude on the view from the room to the garden. Joe Foges of our office proposed that the main window, which can be automatically dropped down like a giant, mechanically operated sash window, be used not only on this conservatory but on the dining room conservatory as well. Although this idea was dropped in the latter room, it gives the spring room its strongest feature, for when the window is completely opened the room resembles a balcony and the framed view of the garden – without any glass or window element – provides a dramatic feature at the end of the long room.

The other half of this ground floor plan was subject to considerable design involvement by the architects since the compressed ceiling form from the study above dictated the plan form below. The structure of the ceiling was not only stepped but was also built on a radial timber construction so that an overlay of the stepping and the sunray scheme was worked into the carpentry construction. The kitchen space was compressed into the lowest part of the room (creating a hard task for the kitchen planners) and we always wanted here to have a window overlooking the adjacent gardens, a solution fraught with problems as this was a party wall overlooking the neighbours' garden. These problems were resolved by indenting the kitchen window back into the room and the centrality of this window together with the lower ceiling in this area divided the autumn and summer rooms in a very formal way.

Jencks had originally thought that the main staircase to the garden should run along the wing of the house adjacent to the neighbouring garden; once we had put forward the idea of two central conservatories, however, the back elevation took on a more symmetrical configuration and it seemed logical to place the staircase in the centre of these two conservatory elements. The design of the stair was worked through with Charles Jencks and Simon Sturgis of our office at a time when Jencks was beginning to take up the reins. The dining room balcony was built in a form almost identical to my very first sketch of 1978. Our contributions to the decoration here were in the brick capitals, radiator columns and sunray patterned ceiling which were all part of the architectural form the decorator inherited. Apart from assisting the kitchen designer from a technical point of view, we had little involvement in the kitchen itself or in the design of the furniture in this or any other part of the house.

THE LOWER GROUND FLOOR ROOMS

These rooms tended to be pushed to the back of one's thoughts and were one of the last things to be finally planned out. The emergence of a dining space under the stairs was a late amendment as a result of Jencks's feeling that the staff room – designed and half built – was rather unsatisfactory. In the rear room, the curved indent of the circular staircase gave rise to a symmetrically placed indent with a bed looking out on the garden. These balanced curved corner sections were designed fairly early on and were repeated in the main bedroom upstairs. Beneath this rear bedroom is the honeycombed brickwork duct leading to the central heat sump under the staircase.

THE ELEVATIONS

The front elevation is a fairly straight interpretation and reworking of the existing house and was never a subject of much dispute between the client and ourselves; the side and particularly the rear elevation were agonised over endlessly as the project developed. In the end the side elevation was the easier to resolve. The two chimneys provided a structure for vertical elements which capped the existing stacks and extended them upwards by a metre. Between them was the Solar Stair, designed as a timber frame construction with a circular roof-light on top. The lead work for the curved annexe roof was particularly well built. One of the trickiest details was the balustrading and the glass between it which had to be adapted in extent due to the District Surveyor's concern about glazing on a party wall. The trellis elements were done by Jencks and indeed the whole design of the facade was very much the result of Jencks and ourselves working together.

The rear elevation was much more difficult, in part because it became apparent earlier on that there was greater freedom at the back of the house to do as one wanted and this itself placed limitations on the collaboration between the Jenckses and ourselves. After our initial agreement on the symmetrical pair of conservatories we went through many, many variations and permutations of detailing and design. We have hundreds of drawings ourselves and I know that Charles Jencks does as well. The eventual scheme of things was in broad concept and shape much as I wanted it to be; the decoration, particularly the classical elements, were very much as Charles wanted them to be.

Drawings to the side elevations
All the early drawings to the side elevations explore the three-dimensional potential of the compressed study roof and how it relates to the windows of the main staircase on the gable wall. Initially, the solutions were fairly formal and conventional – with the two chimneys separated out as vertical elements and the roof curved (at Jencks's suggestion). At the early design stages the resolution of the side elevations seemed to follow a fairly straightforward path, continuing the architecture of the street. However, with the more ambitious final stages of design delicate negotiations with the planners became necessary. Various exploratory studies were made to examine how this lean-to roof interrelated with the kitchen, the garage in the small annexe and the stair-case beyond. It is interesting to compare these drawings and those of the rear elevation with those done by the client, both during and after the stage when his concern was for a decorative language. It is by comparing these drawings that one can see the overlaying of one stage of work onto another and how the collaboration worked.

Elevational study drawings, July and August 1980.

Opposite: Study models of the annexe, August 1980.

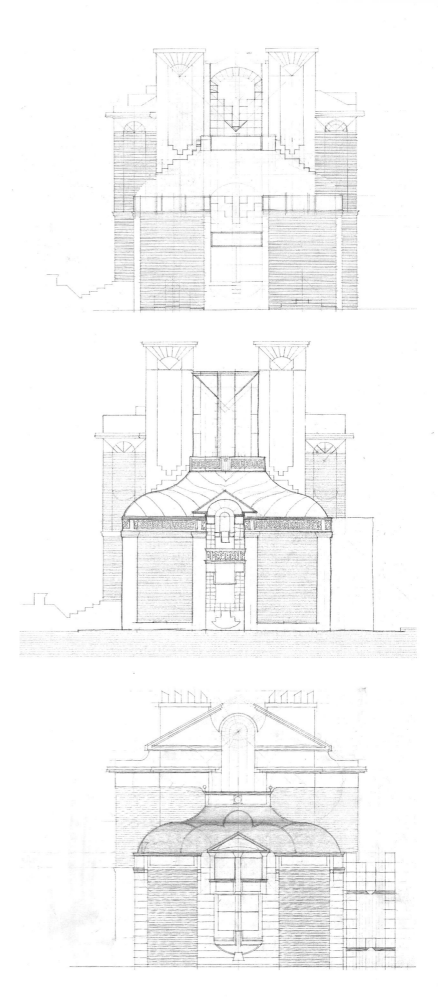

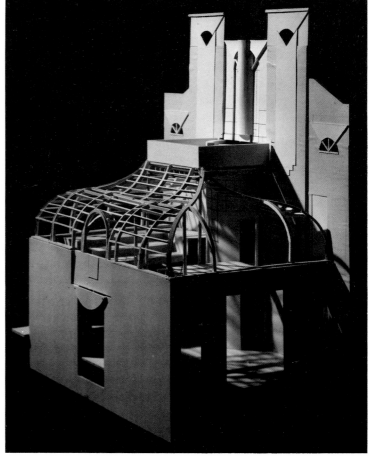

The Models
We continuously built for our own exploration of form several models. These were aimed particularly at resolving the gable and external elevations and their interaction with the spaces behind. But the most interesting feature of the models is that they demonstrate most clearly our search for an interrelationship between interior and exterior forms, that is, the search for the language that would emerge when the plan was expressed three-dimensionally and the inside met the outside. The models were particularly useful on the roof space which at one stage did get over complex.

NOTES ON SPECIFIC SETS OF DRAWINGS

Drawings prepared in April–May 1980 to explain the spatial and construction concepts in the house in order to make a panel for the Venice Biennale.

These drawings were not used in the Biennale because we decided to do a more decorative collage (see below). They were drawn by Tom Politovitz to explain each of the levels and are probably more accurate than any others done at this stage (the conclusion of our spatial work and broad constructional detail). They demonstrate the complexity of the solutions we had arrived at and are unusual for us on this project in that they were prepared in order to explain rather than to build from. We have a scarcity of drawings that are presentational simply because the immediacy of the project was such that very little time was spent on drawings of this type. These drawings are therefore important in presenting the work we had done at this critical stage in the development of the house design. The other drawings which are useful in explaining the surface patterning, both externally and internally, are those done by Charles Jencks, many of which are reproduced in the book *Towards a Symbolic Architecture*. These were usually drawn at the conclusion of our design work and are therefore a good record of

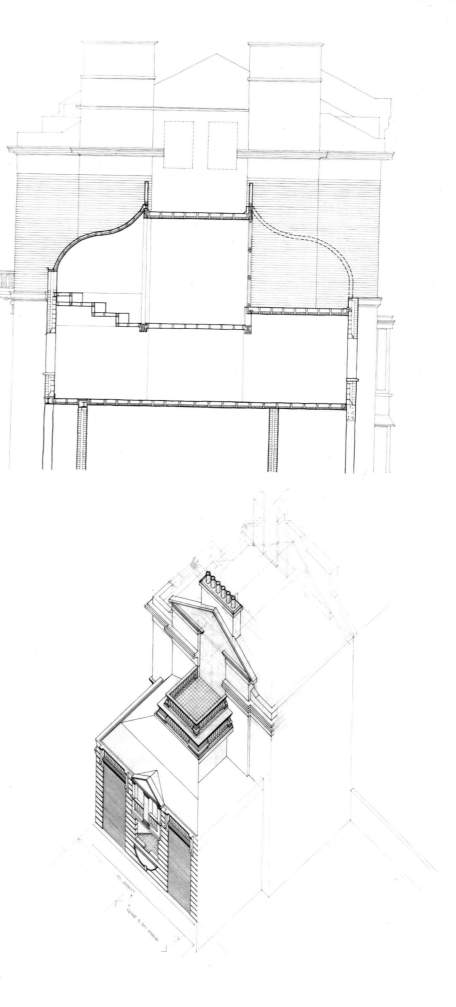

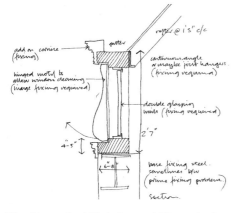

The frieze of rabbit balusters hiding a horizontal window strip was one key design for resolving the external expression of the compressed annexe concept.

what was immediately to be built. It is also worth pointing out that *all* the other drawings in the Jencks book were prepared especially for it; none of the many hundreds of drawings by the Terry Farrell Partnership were published. It is also worth noting that the drawings in the book fairly represent Jencks's particular concern with the surface decoration of the building, a concern which did not significantly penetrate into the spatial and constructional concepts.

Above right: By mid 1980 the interrelationship of construction and spatial organisation was finally resolved. The design of the annexe add-on was the key to the resolution of the entire scheme. *Below right:* Axonometric, January 1979.

Opposite: Development drawings of compressed annexe exterior, January 1979.

Drawings to the rear elevations

Our contribution here was in two main phases. After our proposal for the two conservatories was adopted, we gave rein to a fair degree of experimentation with form. However, a lot of this work was taken up by Charles Jencks for quite a period as he developed his own particular approach to the language of the rear elevation. It then came back to us and we began to work up the reality of the constructional forms for these two conservatories, particularly in so far as their external appearance was concerned. The two squat conservatories were linked so that the rhythm of the facade was ABBA. A staircase splitting the two conservatories gradually developed at ground-floor level and then the idea of a formal staircase emerged during conversations, particularly with Jencks at Cape Cod in Autumn 1980. The solutions proposed by our firm took a wide range of forms and shapes. In the end, I felt that some aspects of the rear elevation are amongst the least satisfactory of all the work on the exterior of the building, particularly at the upper levels where the two big dormers, though successful in themselves, do not relate well to the decorative treatment of the render work below. Due to lots of changes during the construction phase and the continual dialogue between the clients and ourselves, I don't feel that the final resolution of the constructional details, particularly rainwater pipes, was the best that could have been achieved. However, the main staircases work very successfully, particularly the handrail which was developed very much later on in the project when Jencks was working with Simon Sturgis from our office.

Rear elevation studies, January 1979.

Opposite: Rear elevation studies of June (top left) and November 1979 (top right), and November 1980 (below).

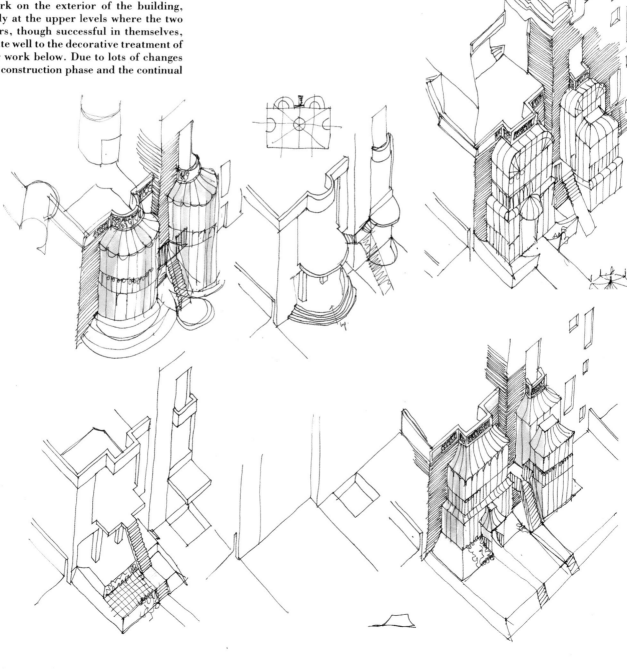

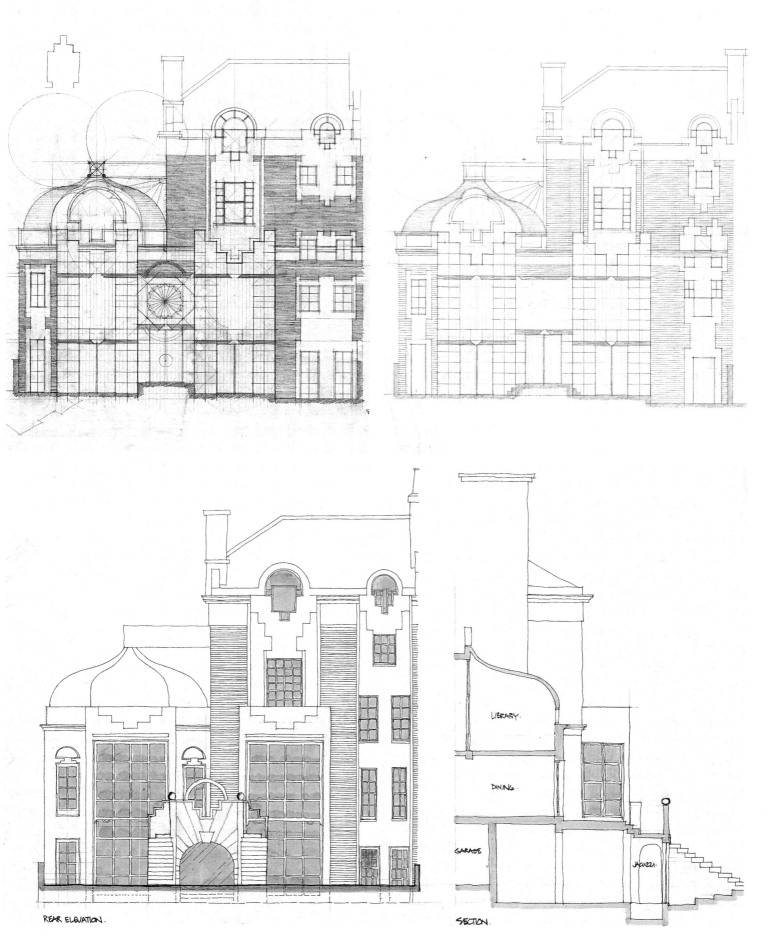

REAR ELEVATION.

SECTION.

LIBRARY.

DINING.

GARAGE

JACUZZI.

Plans at various stages during the development of the design
The plans shown in this article were the only plans drawn between the time of our commission in 1975 and the handover in shell form to our client two-and-a-half years later, except for those drawn specially for the Terry Farrell Monograph. Subsequent plans (as used in *Towards a Symbolic Architecture*) were drawn by others as a result of measuring what we constructed.

Drawings showing constructional details relating to the major elements of the building
The constructional drawings shown in this article were all prepared by the office of Terry Farrell along with approximately 300 more working drawings which were specifically issued to the builders. Constructional detailing was not an isolated activity divorced from design and indeed was very closely linked to space formation and the emerging decorative language.

Terry Farrell's first sketch idea drawings of the new spatial concepts in November 1978
These are only represented in this article in respect of the new conservatories and the interlocking annexe. We regarded the plans presented to us as architects by Jencks at this time as only a little beyond a basic statement of the client's brief. My own sketches, rough as they now seem, contain the essence of the thinking behind the spaces at the rear and side of the house which in essence established the form of the rear and side elevations from this point onwards. At the side, the spatial and constructional organisation emerged as a result of the idea of compressing the study roof downwards into a mansard with its floor interlocking with the dining and kitchen spaces below, with views from one to another. This gave rise to the symmetrical, somewhat pyramidical lean-to roof and the exposure of the two chimneys which now became a major part of the side elevation. The interrelationship of the study and dining room and the views from one to the other and downwards into the lowest floor through the rear conservatory are all expressed in this series of drawings which were sketched immediately before the crucial client meeting when the first ideas were presented.

This series of drawings also shows our proposal that the conservatories be attached only to the lowest two floors rather than being merely vertically stacked bay windows extending individual rooms all the way up the back of the house; that there only be two of them, centrally placed against the two main spaces on the lower floors; and that having enveloped these two lower floors, they establish a spatial dynamic between the two main family rooms at these levels in the very area that divides these rooms from the garden.

Right: Rear conservatory studies, 1979-80.

Opposite above: One of the many rear elevation study models by Terry Farrell Partnership. *Opposite below:* Rear elevation nearing final resolution, February 1981.

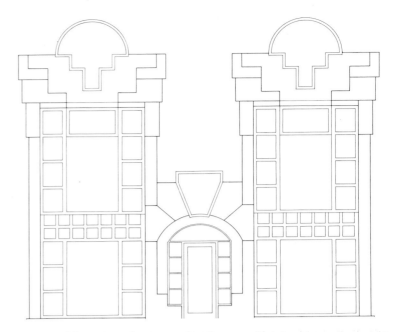

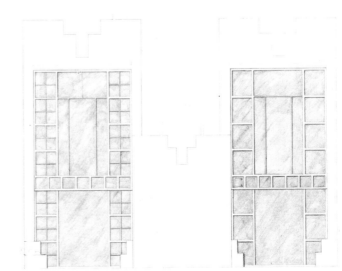

Drawings for the Venice Biennale 1980
This panel, a collage of Terry Farrell Partnership
models, drawings, studies, etc, was prepared as one
of four panels for the Biennale by David Quigley.